Lost Lancashire

The Rusland Beeches line one side of the valley. Once there were over a hundred but age and sickness has reduced their number

Lost Lancashire

The Story of Lancashire-beyond-the Sands

by

A.L.Evans

CICERONE PRESS
MILNTHORPE, CUMBRIA

ISBN 195284 052 8

To Bill and Mary Atkin
who showed us the way

Contents

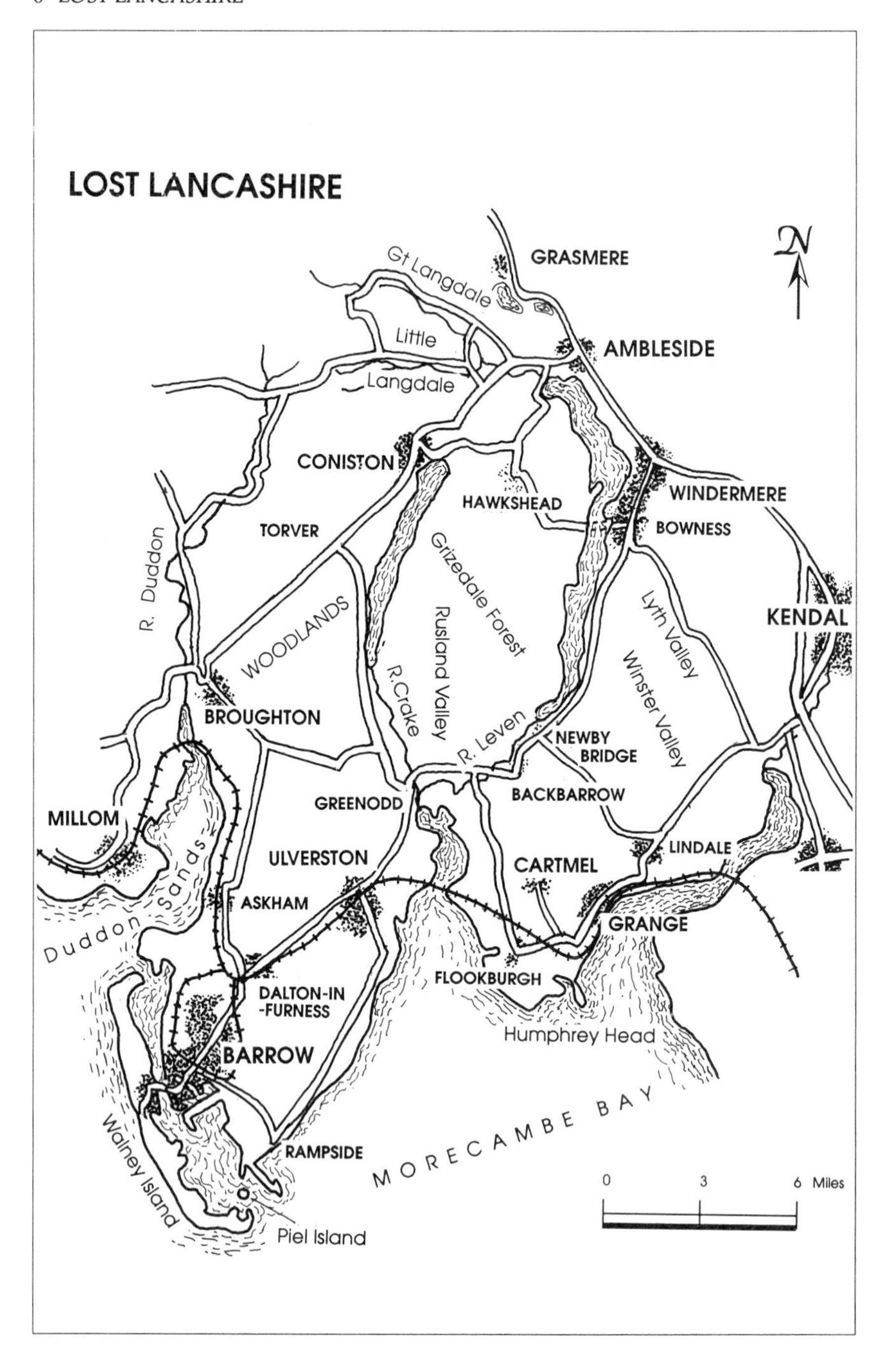
LOST LANCASHIRE
GRASMERE
Gt Langdale
Little
Langdale
AMBLESIDE
CONISTON
HAWKSHEAD
WINDERMERE
BOWNESS
TORVER
R. Duddon
WOODLANDS
Grizedale Forest
Rusland Valley
R.Crake
Lyth Valley
Winster Valley
KENDAL
BROUGHTON
R. Leven
NEWBY
BRIDGE
BACKBARROW
GREENODD
MILLOM
ULVERSTON
CARTMEL
LINDALE
Duddon Sands
ASKHAM
GRANGE
DALTON-IN
-FURNESS
FLOOKBURGH
Humphrey Head
BARROW
MORECAMBE BAY
Walney Island
RAMPSIDE
Piel Island
0
3
6 Miles

1: The Elm River

LOST LANCASHIRE is that part of the Red Rose County known as "Lancashire North of the Sands" until 1974, the year when it was finally and irrevocably lost within the huge new county of Cumbria. In the south of this lovely area, the River Leven, reputably the shortest salmon river in all England, flows out from Windermere, England's longest lake, towards the wide waters of Morecambe Bay. After little more than five miles of travel, the Leven, once part of the eastern boundary of Furness, meets the twice-daily tides moving in and out of the Bay from the Irish Sea.

At the south end of Windermere, where the lake basin overflows into the river, the current passes over the former site of ancient fords where travellers could cross. These ancient crossings, wardened by monks of Cartmel Priory long ago, were finally destroyed in early Victorian times when that part of the lake was deepened for the very first steamer to grace Windermere water. She was the proud and beautiful *Lady of the Lake*, a wooden paddle-steamer with raked masts, tall, graceful funnel, and an exquisitely-carved figure-head borne on a sharply-raking bow. Built for the newly-formed Windermere Steam Yacht Company by Richard Ashburner, a shipbuilder from the creek-port of Greenodd a few miles away, the *Lady* was able to carry 200 passengers. Her first class saloon was bright in pink and white decor; large crystal mirrors were fitted throughout, and these with thick pile 'wall to wall' carpeting added to the air of luxury found aboard this proud little vessel. For these amenities the first class passengers paid 3 shillings to travel from Newby Bridge up the full length of the lake to Ambleside. The others, the second class citizens, occupied the less luxurious saloon and their fare for the same trip was a shilling cheaper.

The *Lady's* keel was laid down at Newby Bridge, on the bank of the Leven below the foot of the lake. She was finally launched from there on July 26th, 1845, with great and clamorous ceremony. Unfortunately, her two tall masts were soon removed; they tangled with overhanging tree branches on her way upstream from her berth at Newby Bridge to the less-confining water of the lake. With a tonnage of less than 50 the *Lady* was 80 feet long, had a beam of 11 feet 6 inches and drew just over 6 feet of water. Her coal-fired engines developed some 20 hp., but she could carry a full load of passengers and steam along at about 8 knots. Her arrival on Windermere, though welcomed by some, was met with both resentment and uproar by many of the local landowning gentry. Jealous of their hitherto undisturbed privacy, they feared that the natural amenities of the lovely lake would be affected, the air polluted by her smoking funnel. Most of all, they detested the thought of day-trippers, whose presence would, they said, vulgarise the area and disturb the peace of the neighbourhood.

Before 1836, there was no regular passenger service of any kind on Windermere. The first such traffic was started by James Gibson who had a grocery business in Ambleside. He was partnered by Mr Samuel White, the proprietor of the Swan Hotel at Newby Bridge. Gibson ran his service from Ambleside by way of the growing village of Bowness. The passengers travelled down the lake to Bowness and crossed to the Ferry Hotel on the west bank. There, they changed to the vessel owned by Mr White and continued on down Windermere, discharging finally at Newby Bridge. Both of these craft were no more than large rowing boats, clumsy, slow, and with little or no protection from any inclement weather.

Nevertheless, both proved popular and in 1843 Gibson, conscious of the growing tourist traffic and the money to be made from it, published *A Guide to the Scenery of Windermere.* In this the passenger service was described: 'There are likewise two boats, daily to Bowness and Ambleside, up the lake a distance of 14 (!) miles; the first Boat leaves Newby Bridge at 8 o'clock in the morning, meeting the one at the Ferry Inn which leaves Ambleside at the same hour; the second Boat leaves each place again at 1 o'clock in the Afternoon, and meets as before at the Ferry. This is a very great accommodation to visitors, as it affords an opportunity of seeing the Lake at light expense, the fare being only three shillings; a private boat to the Ferry Inn is charged five shillings, beside the Boatman, and five shillings to Bowness, the Boatman in such cases expects three shillings, or three shillings and sixpence, as he has no other pay but what passengers give him ...'.

The impending departure of the boat from Ambleside was always announced by the blowing of a horn, and though the journey in rough weather must have been an ordeal for passenger and boatman alike, this passenger service, rough and ready though it was, rarely failed to fulfil its purpose.

The arrival of the *Lady of the Lake*, the first of a long line of steamers, put paid to the Gibson and White service but there was soon intense rivalry of another sort when other steamers appeared. In 1846 the second steamer, *Lord of the Isles*, a replica of the *Lady* was launched with due ceremony. She mysteriously caught fire in 1850 at her Bowness Bay moorings and was burnt out beyond repair. Two local young men were charged with arson but then discharged for lack of evidence. They were thought to be working for the Windermere Iron Steamboat Company, ruthless rivals of the owners of the *Lady* and the *Lord of the Isles.* The two companies were in extreme competition and it is significant that the *Lord of the Isles* was destroyed soon after the second company put their own *Firefly* and *Dragonfly* on lake water.

Trouble between them was still continuing in 1854 when vital engine parts of the *Lady* disappeared and were finally found and fished from the bottom of the lake during her refit! By 1858, after much argument, however, the two rivals had merged into the Windermere United Steam Yacht Company. The final ship built for them was the *Swan*, launched in 1869, but, amazingly, remaining in service until she was finally withdrawn and broken up in 1938. By then, the lake services were run by the L.M.S. Railway Co., who had taken over from the old Furness Railway. British Rail were the next owners, followed by the P. & O. Company. Today the 'steamers' (all of which are now diesel-powered), are owned by a man who also owns the famous and fabled Orient Express; the Windermere Iron Steamboat Company.

Before the arrival of any steamer service the shallows at the southern end of Windermere from Fell Foot on the eastern shore to land now occupied by the present steamer quay at Lakeside (formerly known as Landings) were fordable when the lake-water was suitably low. One of these crossings was labelled Tinkler's Ford in memory of one Tinkler, a travelling, itinerant tinker, come to mend local pots and pans and who, straying from the marked shallows, was drowned in the lake, his body left standing upright, both feet firmly and deeply planted in lake-bed mud! Another ford close by was marked by a giant squared block of white limestone, known as the Cheese-press, which indicated water level. When the block showed above the surface the ford was shallow enough to cross in safety, but when it could not be seen the water was too deep to be waded. A fine arrangement for knowledgeable locals but of little help to any strangers blissfully ignorant of such a simple warning system!

Below the site of these former fords Windermere narrows quickly into the obvious channel of the River Leven, then just as suddenly it widens again, changed briefly into a broad, tarn-like pool. In season this is a delightful, reed-fringed haunt of coot and waterhen, tufted duck and goldeneye, heron and merganser, mallard and other feeding wildfowl. From here the pace of the river water quickens, running rapidly over shallows to swirl under the old and sturdy pillars of Newby Bridge. This 16th century construction, the last bridging point upstream, carries a road now hardly wide enough for a modern car. It has V-shaped bays for pedestrians above each pillar, these originally being made to help those on foot dodge any late-Elizabethan or early Jacobean cumbersome wheeled traffic.

Eventually, with the development of the turnpike roads, traffic included the rumbling stage coaches of the 18th and early 19th century; vehicles such as the *Royal Mail*, or the *New Times*, each a fast four-in-hand. These crossed the bridge twice daily proudly advertising fares of '3/6d inside, 2/6d outside ...' for the journeys to and from Ulverston, 9 miles away.

Such fares were usually too much for poorer folk forced to travel, though in those days, until the advent of the railway, most working men and women rarely travelled far from their own immediate home area unless forced to do so. The crowds of widely-travelled soldiers and sailors returning from the French Wars in Napoleonic times, rapidly disbanded by an uncaring government, and passing through the district in droves, were also far too poor to use either horse or wheeled transport. They, like most, were forced to travel on foot. Earlier still this late Elizabethan bridge, then the best of its kind in the district, carried beggars, tinkers, potters, chapmen (foot-pedlars), other travellers on foot and on horseback, and trains of swaying packhorses - the hardy mules and tough fell ponies plodding steadily over the bridge nose to tail.

Local legend has this site as a busy river-crossing in the first century of the Christian era; for the old story insists that the present Newby Bridge, however ancient its true origin, is built over shallows which once bore a paved Roman ford.

Galava, which means the place by the rushing river, was a busy and important Roman fort at the head of Windermere, where the scanty remains of it may be seen today. It was built early in the second century A.D., and there is little doubt that the Romans ferried goods and material to and from Galava by way of the broad waters of Windermere, rather than use road or track through possible hostile country. The native tribes were not always docile; indeed, a memorial stone discovered in 1963 near Galava is dedicated to a poor company record clerk, 35-year-old Flavius Romanus, 'killed in the fort by the enemy'.

As to the fort there is mute proof of a strong southern connection in its tumbled stones, for some of the Galava masonry is made of a rock quarried near Lancaster; a heavy and awkward material to move by any ancient road. Was it brought over the Bay from Lancaster harbour by flat-bottomed barge, and ferried upstream as far as the tide in the Leven would allow? And then transported by mule (or human muscle) around the falls and rapids of that river, to the first place where it could be put on board ship once more, and finally rowed or sailed up the lake to Galava's quayside at the lake-head? It would seem an obvious route, particularly for awkward or heavy goods, but sadly, there is no surviving documentation or other record to prove any Roman traffic here. Of the supposed Roman ford below the present Newby Bridge the writer has seen nothing, despite several years of looking.

Newby Bridge may be one of several built locally and named by various families. In this case, the bridge was probably the work of the Newbys, an ancient family of Barber Green, a hamlet a few miles down the road to the south. Some of these old bridges, believed to be prefixed by family surname, may well date from the early 17th century, but there are few complete records. Several local examples are Penny Bridge, Spark Bridge and Bowland Bridge; Penny is certainly a local surname, and the bridge records traceable, but of the other two, I can find little.

The *Swan Hotel*, on the north bank of the Leven close by the northern end of Newby Bridge, is today a busy hotel. Little more than a hundred years ago it was a bustling hostelry, a stopping place for the rest and relief of stage-coach and other travellers. The *Swan* was a blessed halt which meant time for relaxation, a chance to stretch cramped legs, to enjoy a drink, or to eat a hearty and welcome meal for all those braving the twisting road over the

The Swan Hotel at Newby Bridge.. A stopping point for the turnpike coaches

eastern fell to and from the 'auld grey toon' of Kendal by way of the switchbacked 1763 turnpike.

Less than sixty years after this innovation, the *Swan* became very busy indeed on the opening of the 1820 turnpike from Lancaster by way of Milnthorpe and Heversham; a safer route which wound through winding country lanes. This new route avoided the dangerous sands of Morecambe Bay, the more usual and often hazardous 'Oversands' crossing between Hest Bank, Cartmel and Ulverston, whenever the twice-daily tides permitted. Though the turnpike added almost 20 miles to the journey between Lancaster and Ulverston it was neither dependent on nor touched by any tidal water. It was, therefore, the route chosen by the more nervous passenger frightened of the Bay crossing.

In more illiterate times (though the literacy of 18th and early 19th century Furness and Cartmel folk was surprisingly good overall), one ancient edict insisted that every inn must bear an easily recognisable sign of its trade. The Newby Bridge *Swan* does just this and more; it carries a large metal effigy of a swan on the lintel of the front door. Above it, jutting from the wall, black, and also metallic, is a large bunch of giant grapes, one of the old indicators of an inn selling wine as well as beer. A further metal pattern of spurs, riding crop, and stirrups, on the wall by the door, is a reminder of the old inn's coaching days. If these were not enough, a living grape vine still creeps up the western half of the front wall. Each successful fruiting, in defiance of the odd English weather, produces bunches of small, sweet green grapes!

Opposite the hotel, on the south bank of the river, a huddle of grey stone buildings crouch near the water's edge. These belong to the old corn mill; no longer busy making flour but still to be treasured for it has a long and time-honoured past. The ancient wooden gearing, the drive from the creaking water-wheel, is more than two centuries old. The building, or one pre-dating it on the same site, was old in the time of Queen Elizabeth I. It was sold in 1609 to an unnamed local entrepreneur by Elizabeth's learned successor; James I of England - James VI of Scotland, son of Mary Queen of Scots.

Other than grinding oats, the rare wheat, or barley, it housed another trade; the miller was an eel-fisherman! He used an eel trap close by the weir which fed the mill wheel with river water. He did this for a few days in the autumn of every year, reaping a rich and wriggling harvest from the churning Leven. This was the time when migrating silver eels, recognised instantly by the breeding dress of mercury-bright belly skin, stirred from Windermere's muddy bed urged on by an age-old call to the breeding grounds far out to sea; somewhere down in the mysterious Sargasso, in the

Waterside House, once the home of Clementina Sobieski Douglas, said to be the illegitimate daughter of Bonnie Prince Charlie

deep and dark of mid-Atlantic water, where millions of these eels congregate far below the surface, at a place never yet precisely located by any man.

Downstream, on the opposite bank, half-hidden in a green hollow, is a tall old building known as Waterside House. Once, it was the home of a 'princess', supposedly the golden-haired, illegitimate daughter of Bonnie Prince Charlie. Her story, if it be true, makes a sad and fascinating tale. In 1771, according to the register of Finsthwaite church nearby, the 'Princess' was buried as Clementina Sobieski Douglas in that churchyard. Some say her real name was Walkinshaw and that her grandfather of that surname was a friend of the dour, morose 'Old Pretender', the self-styled James III of England, father of Prince Charlie, and at the heart of the earlier Scots' rebellion of 1715. Clementina's mother was Clementina Marie Sophie, Walkinshaw's daughter and, when both very very young, this elder Clementina was the constant playmate of Bonnie Prince Charlie. Later on she became his mistress and her daughter, the Clementina Sobieski Douglas of Finsthwaite church record, was supposedly the Prince's child.

After the defeat of the Prince and his Highlanders at Culloden in 1746, followed by his escape to France and subsequent exile, Clementina was thought to be in great danger from the triumphant House of Hanover. She was therefore hidden away for years at Waterside House.

Another fine old farm at Finsthwaite, two miles away, with strong

Jacobite connections goes by the strange name of July Flower Tree, a title that so far has defied all explanation or research. It might be a corrupted version of *Tres jolie fleure:* another place which once housed the illegitimate Clementina, who was the *Tres jolie fleure* (very pretty flower) of her adoring mother, the mistress of Charles. If so, why was Clementina kept here? It may have been the work of the shrewd Dr William Tayler of Oxford, a staunch Jacobite with strong family connections with the ancient Tayler family residing at Finsthwaite Hall. They were all devout Catholics, sturdy Jacobites and followers of Prince Charles but apparently discreet (or lucky?) enough to remain unsuspected by the Hanoverians. All of which makes a marvellous tale; but is it true? Both farms mentioned, Waterside and July Flower Tree, certainly exist and are rather better than the usual farm of that time. Both are expensively panelled, while at Waterside House a stone over the fireplace bears the initials "C.R.A.", which has been suggested as meaning *Charles, Roi Angleterre* though the date is 1675. Whatever the truth - the tale is repeatedly denied by some historians - and apart from all local and other

Charles, Roi Angleterre? A panel in Waterside House. The date is earlier than Bonnie Prince Charlie, who was never king in any case!

legend, a Clementina Sobieski Douglas was quite definitely buried in Finsthwaite churchyard in 1771. Her gravestone is modern, a small white marble cross erected by a romantic and pitying vicar earlier this century. By a shrinking number of local people, the golden-haired Clementina is still referred to as the Princess.

Away from Waterside, over ancient weirs, across foaming rapids and down through rocky narrows in thundering fall, the hurrying Leven slides at last under a narrow packhorse bridge by the new White Water Hotel and Timeshare complex at Backbarrow. Though much altered the huge central building, the core of the original Backbarrow cotton mill, still retains much of the fabric of the former 'Dolly-blue' works where chemicals were prepared for 'whitening the whitest wash'. A few years ago the grey walls of this factory, not to mention the workers themselves, wore a smother of

The White Water Hotel and timeshare complex at Backbarrow. The huge central building was the core of the original cotton mill and later, 'dolly-blue' factory. The powerful current which drove the machinery can be seen clearly

brightest cobalt blue, a colour glorious to the eye, but a product obnoxious to any nose! Frequently the factory chimney reeked of hydrogen sulphide, a smell akin to rotten eggs. It was a stink which was particularly awful when fog and mist hung over the river valley and kept the fumes low.

In the late 18th and early 19th centuries, Backbarrow cotton mill was notorious. It appeared in a terrible light after a government enquiry of 1816 uncovered some of the practices carried out there. The Backbarrow millworkers included 150 parish apprentices, all of them children who were consigned to their employers from the age of seven or eight and held by the factory owners, quite legally, until they were 21! Most of these poor, sad little waifs came from the orphanages of Liverpool or London, forced into a life of drudgery by parish and workhouse masters and various 'boards' eager to alleviate yet more financial pressure on local parish rates.

Life in this and other mills was closely akin to slavery for these unfortunate children. It was not a great deal better for the adult workers. At Backbarrow cotton mill, in the closing years of the 18th century and the beginning of the 19th, circumstances were particularly hard for the children. Their regular working hours, Saturdays included, were from 5 in the morning to 8 at night, with half an hour for breakfast at 7 o'clock and a further half hour for dinner at noon. The children worked the whole time, for there were no seats on which to rest, even for a moment. When the demand for more cotton became pressing they might work even longer, from 5.00 a.m. to 9.00 p.m., without the usual Sunday break, for as long as three weeks on end.

There were two mills, both water-powered. When the river water was low, as in drought, and the water flow insufficient to work both water-wheels at once one mill worked during the day and the other at night. On Sundays many children still had to work from 6.00 a.m. till noon, cleaning and servicing the spinning machines. Whilst the rest were herded to Finsthwaite church, three miles away, where the doubtful virtues of Georgian Christianity, plus perhaps a modicum of reading and writing, were pounded into them by their overseers and a sanctimonious cleric. This reverend gentleman was the man who reported to the Governmental Enquiry of 1816 that '... the children, or apprentices, belonging to the cotton factory of Messrs Ainsworth, Catterall and Co., at Backbarrow, generally and regularly attend divine service in the chapel ... every Sunday when the weather will permit: that during the service they behave with great propriety: they appear neat and clean, and in all respects demean themselves in a descent and orderly manner ... .
P.S. I beg leave to state that out of 150 children, the number employed, there have been only six deaths in the seven last years; and three of these came to the place in a very sickly state and one was drowned by accident ... .'

The local doctor who attended the children was no better: 'I have attended the apprentice house ... at Backbarrow ... upwards of 6 years ...' he wrote 'and that during that time the children have been particularly healthy, and the number of deaths very few. I consider the treatment of the children very good in all respects ...'. The apprentice house stood by the west bank of the river close to the bridge and was pulled down years ago.

At the same time, the overseers and governor of the apprentices reported that ' ... we attend every Sabbath day at the apprentice house ... and accompany the children to Finsthwaite chapel for the morning's service; that in the afternoon we teach them to read in the Bible, New Testament, or Spelling Book, according to their ability, and that every attention is paid to strict observance of the Sabbath ...'

Also at this mill, long before any consciences were stirred enough to think of public enquiry, more terrible events took place. When business economy demanded it, and when there was no work, the children were turned loose on the world, abandoned completely and left to fend for themselves as best they could, possessing nothing but the clothes which they wore. One particularly heartless works' master (but no doubt instructed by *his* masters, the mill-owners) took the children on what was to be a 'picnic' on Flookburgh sands, a few miles away, at the edge of the Bay. On arrival there the children were abandoned completely and told to make their way south, completely destitute, by way of the notorious and very dangerous Oversands Bay crossing.

The frank and chilling report to the Select Committee of the House of Commons, on May 24th, 1816 'On the state of children employed in the manufactories' shows this darker side of the coin. The evidence given by Mr John Moss, Governor of the Preston workhouse, and former Master of the Backbarrow apprentices between February 14th, 1814, and March, 1815, is quoted verbatim below. It makes chilling reading:

> '*Were any children employed in these mills?*
> There were 111 children employed when I went there first, and as many as 150 when I left. All parish apprentices chiefly from London - the parishes of Whitechapel St. James's, and St. Clement's, I think. There was a few from Liverpool workhouse. Those that came from London were from 7 to 11; those from Liverpool were from 8 or 10 to 15.
> *Was there any proportion of idiots among the children?*
> No, none.
> *Up to what period were they apprenticed?*
> One and twenty.
> *What were the hours of work?*
> From 5 o'clock in the morning till 8 at night all the year through.
> *What time was allowed for meals?*
> Half an hour for breakfast and half an hour for dinner.
> *Had they any refreshment in the afternoon?*
> Yes, they had their drinking taken to the mill. Their bagging, they call it.
> *You mean luncheon?*
> Yes.
> *Did they work whilst they ate their afternoon refreshment?*
> Yes.
> *They had no cessation after dinner till 8 o'clock at night?*
> No.
> *At what hour was the breakfast?*
> At 7 in the morning; they came to their breakfasts at 7 o'clock, and then the bell rang for them at half past seven.

Did they leave the mill at breakfast time?
Yes, they always left the mill and came to the house.
What was the dinner hour?
12 o'clock. They returned to the mill at half past twelve.
Did they, beyond working those 15 hours, make up for any loss of time?
Yes, always. They continued working till 9 o'clock, sometimes later.
Did the children actually work 14 hours in the day?
Yes.
And one hour was allowed for the two meals, making 15 hours in the whole?
Yes.

An old water turbine preserved at Backbarrow. The mill was notorious for its treatment of child labour

Was this before the Apprentice Bill, or after?
It was last year, and it is in practice now.
What time did they rise from bed?
I always got them up at half past four to get them ready for the mill by five.
How far was their sleeping room from the mill?
It might not be above a hundred yards, hardly such.
Did they rise at half past four in the winter season?
They were always to be at the mill by 5 o'clock winter and summer, and never late.
Did any children work on Sundays as cleaners of the machines?
Yes, generally every Sunday; I do not know that ever they missed one Sunday while I was there.

How many hours did they work on a Sunday?
Their orders were 6 to 12.
Did you remonstrate against this?
Yes, I did frequently. It was never much better.
Did the masters ever express any concern for such excessive labour?
No.
Would the children sit or stand to work?
Stand.
The whole of the time?
Yes.
Were there any seats in the mill?
None.
Were they usually much fatigued at night?
Yes, some of them were very much fatigued.
Where did they sleep?
In the apprentice house.
Did you inspect their beds?
Yes, every night.
For what purpose?
Because there were always some of them missing, sometimes might be run away, others I have found have been asleep in the mill, upon the mill floor.
Did the children frequently lie down on the mill floor at night when their work was done, and fall asleep before their supper?
I have found then frequently upon the mill floor after the time they should have gone to bed.
At what hour did they go to bed?
Nine o'clock was their hour when they worked the usual time.
In summer time did you allow them to sit up a little later?
Yes, sometimes till half past nine.
Were any children injured by the machinery?
Very frequently. Very often their fingers were crushed, and one had his arm broken.
Were any of the children deformed?
Yes, several; there were two or three that were very crooked.
Were the children fed well?
Yes, very well.
Before your time at Backbarrow Mill, were the children turned out on the high road to beg their way to their former parishes when the former proprietor stopped payment? Were they taken from the mill in a cart, and then turned

adrift near the sands of Lancaster road?
Yes, I was informed they were.
Did you hear that the gentlemen of Lancaster complained of this inhumanity?
Yes.
Were any fetched back in consequence of these complaints?
Yes, I believe they were.
Were they then turned over to Messrs Ainsworth, the present proprietors?
Yes.
After they had served out their apprenticeship to Messrs Ainsworth, were they not compelled to serve extra time, under the pretence that so much time was lost by being turned out on the road, and obliged to go to Lancaster?
Yes, there was one boy out of his time while I was there, and when the day came his master said that he had to serve six weeks, I think, longer, in consequence of his having run away; he said he never had run away, he was turned out, and he had worked at Caton factory and they made him serve that time out ... '.

I wonder what the local vicar and the doctor of that time thought of all this? Did their consciences never stir? It was a particularly brutal age, and perhaps it is unfair to condemn such men out of their time and place. Perhaps, after all, such incidents and such times are best forgotten after all these years? I wonder?

Beyond Backbarrow mill and all its sad child-memories, the river downstream flows by the ruins of an 18th century charcoal-iron works. There is very little left of it today; a few tumbledown buildings and an old furnace, dated 1711 on the cast-iron lintel, though this present structure is really an 1870 reconstruction of the original. Nearby was the workshop and home of 'Iron Mad' John Wilkinson and his father Isaac, both early and innovative iron-founders. Father started by buying molten iron from the works, and taking it rapidly across the road to his own workshop where it was moulded into flat-irons and other domestic appliances. John, when old enough, followed his father but did not remain at Backbarrow very long. He rose in fame and fortune very rapidly; from designer and maker of simple domestic ware John became the rich owner and partner in several busy ironworks in North Wales and the Midlands. He was involved in the building of the first iron bridge at Coalbrookdale with the famous Jonathan Darby. John Wilkinson made the cast iron pipes used in the first efficient water supply of Paris; he built one of the first iron ships and cast and bored many of the cannon used by Wellington in the Peninsular War. He is alleged to have also sold cannon (exported as 'ballast' or 'water-pipes') to America, Holland

The reconstructed charcoal furnace where John Wilkinson began his career as an ironmaster

and France, in 1775, when officially, England was at war with all three of them! Indeed, John Wilkinson was the supreme inventor, technician and entrepreneur in all things iron of his age; he was a great driving force of the Industrial Revolution which so changed the face of Britain in the 18th century.

Downstream from where the famous Wilkinsons once worked, but upstream of the delightful road bridge of 1974, the river boils and curls over in many deadly 'stoppers' along one notorious stretch of rapids. Stoppers are the foaming, natural death-traps avoided like the plague by canoeists braving this wild white-water from time to time.

Soon these fearsome rapids give way to calmer, broader water and eventually, to the wide sands of the estuary. Before that, in several places, the river tumbles over weirs which once sent power to numerous water mills; weirs on which grey wagtails now may flirt with flicking tails and plump and white-bibbed dippers chatter their rattling treble every spring. At Low Wood, near Haverthwaite, the first bridging point upstream, which crosses the hurrying river near the upriver limit of tidal flow, there are traces of haematite, blood red iron ore, in the greasy mud of the river bank. Ugly 'Flatts', bulky, awkward, but surprisingly efficient sailing barges unloaded ore from south Furness here in the early years of the 18th century. Horse and cart carried the ore to an early charcoal ironworks beyond the bridge, and later, to the Backbarrow ironworks further upstream which succeeded this first Haverthwaite enterprise. The heavy ore was taken from the holds of the flatt, the horse-driven carts laboriously filled by women and girls trudging with the haematite along the few yards from riverbank to

Low Wood Bridge near Haverthwaite is the first bridging point upstream on the River Leven. Iron ore was once unloaded here

roadway. They bore the bulky material in wheelbarrows or closely-woven, locally-made 'spelk-baskets' of cleverly-woven wood, held in weary arms: or probably, more often, the women and girls carried the baskets aloft, on cloth-padded heads.

Today, the flat-bottomed, deep-bellied ore flatts are all gone, vanished into history. So are the hard-working girl ore-carriers, the heavy muscled horses, and the sturdy, oak-framed ore carts. In their place, every spring, there are more unusual visitors to this stretch of river, below this old Haverthwaite bridge at Low Wood. They arrive in April; yard-long fish, jawless, and without gills; with gold-rimmed eyes, the long head bearing seven breathing holes on each side. These are sea-lampreys, *Petromyzon marinus*, the 'stone-lickers of the sea' if their scientific title be true. They spawn in gravelly riverbed hollows excavated by the females, the eggs fertilized at once, externally, by milt streaming from the accompanying and excited males. These boneless, cartilaginous fish of remote ancestry are parasites, fresh run from the sea. For several years, whilst in the sea, each adult has preyed on salmon and shark, dolphin and sea-trout, clamping onto and sucking nourishment from their chosen host by tooth-rimmed, circular mouths. Now like homing salmon, they return to ancestral water to spawn and die. Their eggs, successfully fertilized, will hatch out into harmless vegetarians, larval *Ammocoetes*, which will live in the river for several years before changing finally into the parasitical adult and heading for the open sea.

Downstream from Low Wood the swollen Leven runs silent and deep. The dark water plays host to many things both above and below the shining surface; particularly to saw-billed, raggy crested mergansers, trout and salmon fishermen par excellence, a species now enjoying a population explosion on this and other Cumbrian rivers. Eager devourers of salmon parr, their presence under the full protection of the law, evokes loud and constant protests from the salmon and trout fishermen.

After a few hundred yards more of swift and glittering flow, but only at the tide's ebb, the river spills out onto gleaming sand. At full tide this is covered, and the fresh river water meets the push and heave of the salty, incoming sea. Half a mile further on, approaching the village and former harbour of Greenodd, the Leven estuary broadens, turning briefly north-west in a wide, smooth sweep, to meet and mingle finally with the clear rushing water of its smaller sister, the River Crake.

Sea lampreys on the gravelly spawning beds, female in the foreground

2: Beside The Rocky River

REMARKABLY, THOUGH MANY of the place-names hereabout are in the language of the Vikings, the titles of the rivers Crake and Leven appear in the old Welsh tongue. The Crake, for example, may be part of an original Welsh Afon Creic, the rocky stream; the Leven corrupted from the Cymric llwyf, meaning elm tree. This was the language of the 'Compatriots', who between Roman departure in early 400 A.D., and full and complete Saxon conquest by the mid-10th century, managed to occupy an area reaching from Chester northwards into present-day Dumbartonshire. The Compatriots were Celtic people of a kingdom separated from old Wales by early Saxon invasion. They spoke the same language, had a similar culture, and were virtually a north-western extension of the proud Cymri, the true Welsh.

These men of the north, the Compatriots, were the 'Strathclyde Welsh', split apart from Wales by the Saxons in the 7th century A.D., but ever aware of their ancient Welsh roots. They were the most ancient of Britons, living here long before and long after the Roman interlude. Some were the folk of legend, like Artos, the Bear; a man trained in disciplined Roman methods of warfare. As a cavalry commander and sworn enemy of the Saxon hordes, operating from 'merrie Carlisle' he became our own King Arthur, our national hero of deathless fame!

Though the old Celtic Leven means Elm river, that tree species has long gone from the banks of the wild stream, but Crake - stony river - is an appropriate title for water flowing over such a spate-scoured and rocky bed. Such Celtic river titles do appear from place to place in Cumbria, but the rivers flow over a landscape speckled and spotted with place-names given by later invaders; labels attached in blunt Saxon on the richer seaward fringes and the best arable land, or in gruff old Norse, usually about the bleaker, harder-won upland areas. Surprisingly, a few Cumbrian mountains and hills, and some villages, also retain their old Welsh titles. So does the town, Penrith, in north-east Cumbria, a name which means simply, the red headland.

At Greenodd (the Groen-oddi, the green headland named by some forgotten Norseman) the River Leven loses much of its identity as it merges with the clear fast water of the River Crake, a turbulent stream draining Coniston Water, some 9 miles upstream to the north. Beyond Leckbarrow

Point, a tall crag of weather-riven slate crowned by leaning, wind-sculptured Scots pines, the two rivers combine, making the estuary widen still more.

The joining of the two rivers at Greenodd has created a marvellous area for bird-watcher and botanist alike. As a further bonus, the silting started by the building of new road bridges has evolved into a miniature salt-marsh; a fascinating triangle of smooth mud, sea-washed turf and scattered halophytes, which are plants best able to resist poisoning by tidal water. Scurvy grass, which is not a grass but a member of the Crucifereae, the cabbage and turnip family, is one. It shows snow-white flowers in late March or April. This fleshy-leaved, bitter tasting plant is chock-full of vitamin-C, and owes it common English name to sailors of an earlier age, who chewed the leaves, or made 'tea' from them to offset the deadly gum-rotting disease of scurvy; so prevalent on every long sea voyage, when the crew and passengers went short of fresh fruit and vegetables. Another old salt is *Chenopodium*, (Goosefoot), so-called by the leaf-shape. One of this family - an allied species formerly cultivated as a vegetable but now regarded as a weed - is 'Good King Henry'. Relished by any free-ranging farmyard poultry, it is also known as 'Fat Hen', and was once encouraged, not destroyed as an unwelcome plant-pest. Pollen analysis proves that the first seeds of this plant came to this country from the Continent. They arrived with the first English farmers of all, a Neolithic people of some 4,000 years ago; a fact which makes me treat this so-called weed with something akin to reverence.

According to wind, weather and season, the Greenodd lay-by, at the edge of the busy A590 east of the turnoff for Coniston, may make a marvellous bird-watching platform, particularly for seeing waders and wildfowl. Birds as diverse and as magnificent as Icelandic whooper swan and Scottish greenshank may appear. I have seen Canada and greylag geese, sandpiper and kingfisher, cormorant and teal, mallard, merganser, goosander, and goldeneye here at the appropriate time of the year, as well as a veritable host of other species, ranging from pebble-eyed shag to sweet-voiced goldfinch.

In late July, unusual flower species such as primrose-yellow, sweet-smelling melilot appear, side by side with tall, bright hyacinthine spikes of the uncommon but very beautiful blue sow thistle. Both are field escapes, regarded by farmers as pests of cornfield or meadow. Crow garlic (waxy-leaved, with strangely shaped flowers of heliotrope and a rank smell of onions), sweet wild sage, nectar-laden purple heather and bright-eyed, brilliant yellow hawkweeds sprout from the shattered rock of Leckbarrow Point. Overlooking the saltmarsh it towers above a fringe of soft-leaved hazel, loaded every autumn with fat white nuts. There's elderberry too, black with bead-like, purple-staining fruit.

In late spring, back east along the A590 about two hundred yards, a steeply sloping cottage meadow is smothered each year in small, self-sown native wild daffodils. There are so many of them that hardly a finger can be put between the bright golden flowers.

In late summer, the roadside strips show a brighter yellow; a deeper shade than daffodil, belonging to masses of sweet-scented corn marigolds. Until quite recently *Chrysanthemum segetum* was a cornfield weed, a rapidly vanishing species almost eliminated by the development of seed-screening and various selective herbicides. It too is a plant of ancient origin; possibly first appearing here with the Late Bronze Age peoples. More likely, it advanced northwards with the legions of mighty Rome. Who knows? Perhaps the first corn marigold seeds escaped from sacks of unscreened Roman corn going to feed the garrisons along the straight Roman roads. These roads were built on 'aggers' or railway-like embankments over marsh and hollow, the fresh soil of which provided such ready and newly formed seed beds for the beautiful plant invaders. Unfortunately, the Greenodd marigolds have no such Roman origin; the seeds came in red soil dumped here during road alteration, most likely, judging by the colour, from the iron-bearing soils of south-west Cumbria.

At the edge of river and saltmarsh, immediately before the Crake meets the Leven, the neat and kitten-like footprints of questing, bloodthirsty mink have replaced the former broad and welcome pad-marks of playful otters. Gaunt herons stalk here, and leave giant three-toed impressions in the soft mud alongside the tiny prints of grey wagtail or the huge webs of mute swans. At low tide, ragged cormorants spread untidy wings to dry after fishing the river channels, each a dark and rather sinister silhouette on the whalebacked sandbanks. A flock of some 300 peewits takes up residence on Greenodd sands every winter, and at the same time, a wisp of teal, Britain's smallest native duck species, may feed in the bed of the river after every tide. Carrion crows are never far away; like the gulls, which may include the common, black-headed, herring and lesser blackbacked species, as well as the bass-voiced, goose-sized

Mink tracks at Greenodd

The 1820 New Bridge over the Crake at Greenodd

greater black back (a magnificent bird aptly titled 'Copsyn y Mor', the grand Sea Chief by the more romantic Welsh).

Dippers, the plump 'Water Blackbirds' of the faster hill streams and rivers, whirr up and down the Crake river-mouth on stubby wings, passing and re-passing under the dark arch of the New Bridge. The name was given in 1820, when it was built to carry the coaches and other traffic of the new Lancaster turnpike over the foaming river. At present, it has been overlaid and strengthened by a new Bailey bridge, prior to the building of a brand new structure downstream.

Until a century and a half ago, before the railways arrived and destroyed it, Greenodd was a thriving harbour, a creek-port of Lancaster. It was also a shipbuilding centre, with three yards turning out sturdy sailing vessels of up to 200 tons burden in its prime. Unfortunately, there appears to be no complete list of all the ships built at Greenodd, but there are a few interesting records of some, like those of the *James*, named after her captain, James Storey. She was built for the North American trade, shipping raw cotton to the infamous Backbarrow and other local mills. James Storey was a giant of a man - more than 25 stones in weight. He could not squeeze through the narrow doors of his new command, so the understanding owner, a Mr Winder, of Liverpool, had all the ship's doorways altered to admit James' huge bulk. Storey's previous ship was the sturdy little *Ant*, a small and useful coaster owing her name to the nest of ants found in her timbers when on the stocks in the builder's yard!

Another interesting local vessel was the *Gummers How*, which was named after a steep fellside on the east side of Windermere, alongside the 1763 Kendal turnpike. The *Gummers How* was made largely of larches felled on that roadside slope, and surprisingly, there is a whole series of reminders of the Greenodd ship on that very hill. These are best seen when the sun is low - as in the early morning, or in the evening, when it westers. The lumps and bumps are more obvious in light snow, or heavy hoar-frost, when dozens of grassy hummocks become obvious in such lighting conditions. About a foot or so in height, perhaps two or three feet in diameter at most, I believe that these hillocks mark the former tree stumps of larches felled for the *Gummers How* vessel. Over the years, these hummocks have been invested by ants, building nests by almost every sawn-off stump, and as the stump-wood rotted, changing it to the fine soil of ant hills which were built, by accident or design, to receive the maximum amount of sunshine! Now, grassed over and often unoccupied, they remain as indelible memorials to a fine vessel built by a busy little port in the 'Lost Lancashire' of long ago!

Another Greenodd ship, the ugliest of all, was the strictly utilitarian *Elephant*. Built in the early 1800s, she was shaped like a giant rectangular box with little regard for beauty and even less for difference between bow and stern. The design was deliberate, for, with an

The Old Post Office, Greenodd. The hinged window, top left, was where mail was handed out to the 11pm coach - the postmistress could then go straight back to bed

interchangeable bowsprit, used at the most favourable end of the ship according to the wind and circumstance, she could sail either way! Bow could quickly become stern, and vice-versa as each occasion demanded. Despite her uncharacteristic ugliness and lack of line, the *Elephant* worked local water for many years before being finally broken up, and made into firewood sold in Ulverston.

Greenodd was very busy indeed in its late 18th and early 19th century heyday. When the 1820 turnpike, coming overland from Lancaster was completed, it became livelier still. One small house in the main street, the village post-office in those days, bore a simple reminder of this until quite recently. In the front of the house, a first-floor bedroom window pane was altered so that it swung outwards like a small door. When the night mail coach passed through at about 11.00 p.m., every weekday, the postmistress leant out from her bedroom window and placed the mail straight into the coach-driver's hands. She could then go straight back to bed!

The list of imports and exports associated with this thriving village-harbour in those days shows great quantity and variety. Up to the middle of last century it included tons of copper ore, ferried down Coniston Water from the mines beyond the lake-head. Gunpowder was another export, from Haverthwaite, loaded carefully on the shore opposite Greenodd after being stored in a purpose-built powder house over there. It arrived by horse and cart, and one wonders if the sweating horses wore huge, padded-

The old powder store at Nibthwaite. Did it suffer an explosion?

leather overshoes as they tramped down the long lane from the gunpowder mills? Examples of such monster boots, formerly used on cart-horses transporting gunpowder to local granite quarries, hang on the wall of the *Horse and Farrier* inn at Threlkeld, near Keswick, to the puzzlement of many customers. Did the horses travelling to Greenodd wear similar shoes, or were brass or copper-nailed leather or wooden horseshoes considered safe enough when the horses came from Haverthwaite to the powder house? Later on more powder, bound for Greenodd (or Ulverston), was ferried down Coniston Water from another large and busy works at Elterwater, in Great Langdale, and stored temporarily *en route* in a building in Nibthwaite woods, well clear of the nearby hamlet at the foot of the lake. Today, only one wall of this powder house remains. Whether the rest of the building fell down with age, or was blown apart by its former volatile contents, I do not know! It does explain why the dangerous powder was always treated with such care, and, in each case, kept well apart from Nibthwaite and Greenodd houses!

Limestone, quarried from Skelwith Rocks, the low white cliffs on the shore opposite to Greenodd, went to a rapidly-growing Liverpool. So did the burnt limestone from the Greenodd kilns, slaked and dried, for use as field fertilizer, or smooth plaster and mortar base in the building trade of Merseyside. Woven oak 'spelk' baskets, made in nearby Sparkbridge, were sent out by the hundred, to serve the potato and vegetable merchants of the Fylde and Ormskirk districts across the Bay. Coal merchants used them in south Lancashire and on the Yorkshire border, and more were used in coaling Liverpool ships, the fuel carried basket by basket into the holds of these early coal-fired steamers. The spelk baskets had many uses. They were woven so closely, with never a nail or a drop of glue near, that they could be used to carry water and never leak a drop!

Another busy trade, now long forgotten, was hoop-making. These wooden rings went to Liverpool by the thousand, where they were used in the West Indian trade to bind the timbers of massive hogsheads. It was an ingenious arrangement; on the way out these hogsheads carried Lancashire coal. Homeward bound, they brought Caribbean sugar! One wonders if they were cleaned between voyages?

Heavy duty chains, probably cannon, cannon-balls, and chain-shot (used to bring down ships' rigging), made upstream on the Crake at Sparkbridge were almost certainly exported from Greenodd in the first half of the 18th century. Roofing slate from Coniston and Tilberthwaite quarries were sent out by the hundred tons to feed the seemingly insatiable demand in the rapidly expanding Lancashire mill towns. Oak bark, expertly stripped

Ann Hodson's beer-house at Pennybridge, later the Sun Inn. A coach stop on the 1763 Kendal-Ulverston turnpike, the first meeting of the Turnpike Trust was held there.. The mullioned windows have recently been restored after being bricked up for many years

in the woods from oak saplings, and rich in tannin, was shipped to southern tanneries. Some still goes from the local woods to feed a trade dealing in luxury leather, but it is now supplied by one man only. The local barking trade will vanish when he retires, a position far removed from the busy days of long ago, when oak barking was so long and commonly established hereabouts that it gave us the old and still well-known Furnessian surname of Barker. Other Greenodd exports were various kinds of chemicals; made almost on the quayside, though no trace of any such works now remains.

Imports to Greenodd were equally varied. Sugar, raw cotton, coal, tobacco, West Indian rum, wine for the local squire, fine furniture for him and the 'quality' and Baltic or Scandinavian timber, were all landed on the quayside. The wood was cut and shaped in the Greenodd sawmills, and some of it was used to build the very first wagons for the early Victorian Furness Railway. Other timber came from America, brought by larger sea-going vessels with too deep a draught to venture across the sandbanks and up the winding river channels of the estuary to Greenodd. In such cases the baulks of timber were dumped overboard outside Barrow, made up into crude rafts, and poled up the Leven estuary, on the next incoming tide, by a voluntary and adventurous crew of three men!

Today, the scanty remains of a wharf, and the existence of the *Ship Inn* (once a warehouse on the busy quay) are two of the very few reminders left of Greenodd's involvement with ships and the sea. Virtually all semblance of the busy, one-time creek-port of Lancaster has been swept away so thoroughly that it is hard to believe that it ever existed. The harbour has long gone; the village remains, but now not much more than a dormitory for those who work elsewhere.

A few yards upstream of the New Bridge of 1820, the river water tumbles over a stony weir at low tide. On the flow, it disappears under the flood, the stream beyond becoming deeper and smooth, a canalised stretch leading to another and older bridge built by the local Penny family in late Elizabethan times. Not surprisingly, this is called 'Pennybridge', which gave its name to the village a few hundred yards up the hill to the west, on drier ground. Close by, on the eastern bank, is an old building once known as *Anne Hodson's beer-house;* probably later glorified into the *Sun Inn*. It bears 17th century window frames called mullions, recently re-discovered after being bricked up for many years, and by the front garden wall there is an 18th century milestone bearing the cryptic legend '17'. This records the distance to Kendal, the weathered stone being a relic of the 1763 Kendal/Ulverston/ Ireleth turnpike. It is one of a dozen such markers still surviving along the old route. From the Greenodd milestone, the winding, narrow track rears savagely uphill, a sharp reminder of one of the trials and tribulations endured by any turnpike coachmen, waggoners or indeed any traveller using this switchback road.

The river section between the two turnpike bridges was straightened and deepened to take incoming ore boats in the early 18th century, before the 1820 New Bridge appeared. These early ore barges sailed over the tide-submerged weir to tie up at the wharf immediately below Pennybridge. From there, the iron ore, which was the rich haematite from Low Furness, was unloaded into horse-drawn carts and taken to the foundry some 200 yards uphill from the quayside. This place made many iron artefacts; for part of its short history, it was involved in making cannon-balls and chains. When the ore cargo was unloaded, it was replaced with manufactured iron goods, the ship then ready to leave on the next convenient tide. It was a neat and business-like arrangement, but the Pennybridge foundry did not last very long and finally closed in 1742.

The selfsame Pennybridge wharf, of neat grey slate and still in pristine condition after more than 200 years of seasonal river spates, tides, wind and weather, once held a more sinister and terrible landed cargo. According to folklore, black slaves were brought from Liverpool to await further onward transportation and re-sale at some disgusting and degrading slave auction. One supposed destination was Storrs Hall, a large mansion (now a modern hotel) on the east bank of Windermere, just inside the border of the former county of Westmorland. In the late 18th century, a male slave in prime condition might bring as much as £45 at an auction, which was a lot of

Above: Little Langdale tarn
Below: Duddon Forge

Above: Penny Bridge - once a hive of industry
Below: Piel Castle

Pennybridge - there was a quay on the right where slaves were landed and cannon balls exported

money in those days. Such ready profit may explain why a certain Sir John Ledgard, the Yorkshire baronet who built Storrs Hall in 1790, was so busy in this wicked trade. Local tale insists he smuggled his slaves into the cellars of Storrs Hall before sending them off to clients elsewhere. Colonel Bolton, who took over the Hall in 1806, was also a slaver who made his fortune in what was cynically called The West Indian Trade, a business which dealt with slaves, rum and sugar in that order. Colonel Bolton, who never served in the army proper, but got his title by equipping a company of Liverpudlian volunteers during the threat of Napoleonic invasion, was a ruthless man. He killed one man in a duel, and a tale told of him when he resided at Storrs Hall recalls a terrible act and a female slave's curse. This curse was 'set by a native woman' thrown into Windermere for some unspecified reason, and whom when '... trying to swim after Bolton's boat ... having her hands cut off by his cutlass ...'! Because of this curse, the Pattinson family of

Windermere refused point blank to buy the Hall when offered it; they took the land but left the building strictly alone! Further evidence of any local involvement in the slave trade is scant, but 'Raselas Belsfield, an Abyssinian slave' is buried in Bowness churchyard, and a certain Molly Kendal, a Negress (and probable slave) died in Pennybridge in 1772. Captain Fayrer, who built Harmony Hall in Milnthorpe, was a retired slaver and Bryan Christopherson, of Pennybridge, whose descendants still live in the district, was importing slaves into Liverpool in 1753, in shiploads of 200 a time!

Today, no trace exists of any former cargo of human misery by the lovely old bridge beside the Crake. Nor is there much left of the former heavy iron industry. The old forge buildings of 1748 remain, but with furnace and machinery long gone. Left behind, as a mute reminder, are the mossers; gas-bubbled lumps of dark red iron slag on the Pennybridge wall, and marking other wall-tops near the old foundry and at the entrance to Pennybridge village. Furnace bricks from the vanished forge top the wall by the Crake's wooden footbridge upstream. The water-powered cotton mill which replaced it has also vanished, betrayed by a stone-lined leat, or water-channel, a careful piece of hydro-engineering running from the river weir to the twin water-wheels. There is also a rotting sluice gate, which controlled

The village of Pennybridge with the road leading to the River Crake

Lumps of iron slag from the old foundry, known as 'mossers', were built into the walls

the water-flow to the huge wheels.

Half a mile upstream of Pennybridge is the hamlet of Sparkbridge, a most marvellous name for a place also once involved in ironworks! It is probably named after a long-vanished family called Sparks, who may well have established a very early iron foundry and chain-making forge on an island in the nearby river. Today, nothing of this is left other than a riverside beach of glassy and cindery slag below the old bridge; old furnace material washed downstream by past river spates. The Sparkbridge forge was busy for more than a hundred years before giving way to a bobbin mill, which churned out wooden bobbins of all sizes for the Lancashire cotton mills. Local wood was used, much of it birch, turned and shaped on water-powered lathes. Later on, in the late 1890s, power for the lathes and electric light came from two giant Gilkes water turbines, made by a Kendal firm still in business today, and famous the world over. The elegant Sparkbridge turbines used the fast-running Crake water, but it was all in vain. Bobbins for a vastly decreased and shrunken industry can be made more easily and much more cheaply in plastic. Senseless and prohibitive charges made by the then North West Water Authority for river-water usage (charges enforced by Government Act) were the last straw; the Act, and the charges, are now altered, but much too late to save what was once a unique local rural industry. The magnificent turbines, superb examples of Victorian skill and invention, were broken up for scrap when the mill finally closed a few years ago! The bobbin mill site has now been developed into flats and summer residences.

The fast-flowing Crake was father to several other water-powered industries along its nine-mile banks. These included corn, cotton and flax mills as well as those making wooden pill boxes, or sawing timber and turning and shaping wood. One water-powered mill, well up river near Nibthwaite, was involved in making small-arms at the time of the 1745 Scots rebellion! Now, none of these are left; indeed, one of the biggest and best is no more than a large grassy mound. It lies hard by a farm with the strange map title of Little Richard; but better known to generations of local folk as 'Mucky Dick's'!

These Crake river-industries have come and gone; none are now left by this delightful stream. Any scars left by such works of man - some of them included amongst the first stirrings of the great Industrial Revolution - are changed out of all original form. Some are long healed-over; the riverside grown and changed back to days of undisturbed peace. Nibthwaite iron foundry, the small-arms factory of yore, is now a prim private house with no trace of the musket, ball-shot, or cannon-ball once made there!

Almost at the head of the river, by Allen Tarn, (which is not a true tarn but merely a widening of the young stream flowing from Coniston Water), there are the remains of yet another riverside quay. This one was made to accept loads of Coniston roofing slate, and mountain copper ore, ferried down the lake for onward transport by road to Greenodd. Now the shattered wharf is nothing more than a tumbled wall of slate, half-fallen into the clear river water. Gunpowder from the works of Elterwater was unloaded here; as already stated, it was stored in the woods beyond. Clear of all human habitation, the mouldering ruins of the old powder house can still be seen. The one wall remaining is bedded down on a sweet-smelling carpet of woodruff, well away from the house-cluster of Nibthwaite village.

Apart from all these past industries, and largely undisturbed these last two centuries, is the Crake river section near Bouthray bridge, half a mile south of Nibthwaite. Old enough to record a repair in 1770, it is another haunt of the chubby dippers, fishing regularly in the gravelly shallows immediately upstream, or whirring down river on wings which seem absurdly small for such a plump body. In summer dusk, the bats and late flying swallows haunt the near-silent stream like so many large moths, the smooth water ringed by drinking swallow or rising trout. On the whole length of this lovely river, I know of no more tranquil, serene place; where one may lean on lichened bridge parapet, relax, and for a while, do little else but simply stand and stare.

Away from this peaceful stretch, south along the road towards Greenodd,

Bouthray Bridge, near the river head

is the hamlet of Blawith (pronounced Blarrth, which is old Norse for 'the dark woodland'). The former forest of sombre trees to the west no longer exist, replaced by a sea of bracken and a spider's web of fell tracks, but the ruin of an old church remains, and there's a newer one recently 'mothballed', no longer in use. The older church and the people once attending in its prime, became the subjects of a mocking rhyme nearly 200 years ago. In the late 18th century, the Blawith villagers decided to build a steeple on the old church, in order to house a bell they wished to buy, for they had nothing else to summon them to church. Blawith was an impoverished hamlet, mostly of poor fell farmers, but they did have a portion of very poor land they could sell. This was Blea Brow, half rock and half starved grass, close by Coniston Water, which the eager Blawithians promptly sold to a local farmer. With the money, they built the church tower, as the old parish records reveal: ' ... the steeple ... to be 10 yards high ... to hold a bell ... John Benson and Roger Atkinson to do the walling ... finding stone and mortar ... except for freestone (usually sandstone) ... at 2s 2d (11 pence in modern money!) a yard ...' The two men were paid this sum for each portion of wall 'a yard high and a yard long ...' . The same parish record also states that the 'chapel wardens to find timber, slate, and other material ...'. When the new tower was finished, the Blawith bell was proudly installed, much to the derision of other folk in the Crake valley. An unknown wit promptly wrote the following lines, still quoted enough today. It reads as follows:

Blawith poor people,
An auld church and a new steeple,
As poor as hell,
They had to sell,
A bit of fell,
To buy a bell,
Blawith poor people!

This happened in 1782, and unlike so many stories and folk tales around the valleys of Crake and Leven, it happens to be true. Ironically, the church which was built later, down the hill and across the road in late Victorian times, now has the original bell from the old steeple installed in comparatively new housing. Yet, with falling numbers of churchgoers, and the necessary re-organisation of the Crake valley churches, this 'new' church is no longer open for use. The Blawith bell, obtained only after such determination amongst 18th century farm poverty, is silent at last. Sadly, it is likely to remain so for a long time to come.

This sad story of the Blawith folk of former years, their bell and their hard-won building of the steeple, is almost a parable. It is a simple and yet stark reminder of a cycle of triumphs and setbacks suffered by so many people over the centuries along the banks of the hurrying River Crake. In the long view, it is a long turnover of valley people and their industries along the short length of the Crake. A centuries-long cycle, in which man is busy by the rushing water for a while, and then, with all his proud works, vanishes for a time. It has been so since the first Norseman ventured up here from the Bay more than a thousand years ago, and set up his farm. I wonder what will happen here in the next millennium?

Unaware of all this, the mindless but lovely river keeps on; speeding down to the sea along its rocky and narrow bed. Unmindful of man and all or any of his works, the Crake continues on its way; as it has done for so many of the long, long years, both long before, and since, any human tried to use its power, or settle on its bonny banks.

3: The Town Below The Lighthouse

ULVERSTON AS A PLACE-NAME is quite mysterious. The suffix ton, from the old English tun, means settlement; one which may have ranged in size from a solitary small farm to a collection of buildings almost a village in size. Thus, the original Ulvers-tun may have been the tun, or farmstead, of a Saxon called Wulfa, or Wulfhere. Just as likely, it might have been the former holding of one Ulfarr, a man of undoubted Scandinavian origin judging by the spelling of his name. Possibly he was one of the many Norse-Irish fleeing from the wrath of the Norwegian king, Harald Fairhair, (or Finehair) in the very late 9th or early 10th century A.D., when that doughty monarch was determined to bring all western Norse settlements under his control. Such places included the Viking settlements of the Western Isles, the Isle of Man, and probably Dublin and any other Irish centres occupied by Norsemen. This caused great alarm and despondency in these places, and eventually, a quick and frantic dispersal of many people to the north-west coast of England, particularly to those parts now in modern Cumbria. The multitude of place-names with strong Norse-Irish influence, and those suggesting Irish settlement (such as Ireleth, in Low Furness, which means the hill slope of the Irish), present on the western seaboard of Cumbria, is certainly not proof of Cumbrian settlement by these second and third generation Irish Vikings; but surely, is it not strong supporting evidence of a massive Norse-Irish influx?

For example, in the valley of the River Duddon, there is a hamlet called Hall Dunnerdale. This is termed a Norse-Irish inversion, the name being written in inverse order; in the true English pattern, it would be Dunnerdale Hall. Another prime example in Furness is Kirkby Ireleth, which again in the old English fashion would be written as Ireleth Kirk. There are many more examples of similar inversions throughout Cumbria, ranging from place-names such as Kirksanton, near Millom, a title meaning St. Sancta's Church (fittingly, St. Sancta is an Irish saint!) to Kirkandrews. Kirksanton is in the south-west of the county, but Kirkandrews (St. Andrew's Church) is in the far north of it, lying beside the northern River Esk, beyond Carlisle, on the Scots border. More Irish influence is present in the Furness place-names of Torver near Coniston, and Biggar, a village on Walney Island. Here, the suffixes 'er' and 'ar' are corrupted 'loanwords' borrowed from the old Irish 'airigh', meaning a shieling, or humble dwelling. Two more local

Hoad Hill monument built in 1855 to commemorate Sir John Barrow

examples are Bethecar a moor east of Coniston, and Stewnor, part of the name of a farm on Kirkby Moor. So it is possible that the man Ulfarr (if he ever existed) came first to that place in all humility! Not as a rampaging, bloodthirsty, all-conquering Viking, but sheepishly, perhaps; with a boatload of fellow Norse-Irish, fleeing from Ireland to Cumbria. All of them humbled refugees; sheep men, perhaps, ready to work poor, previously unsettled uplands, desperate to escape the wrath of a Norwegian king! Perhaps, after arrival, he acquired the original Ulverston farmstead by marrying into an established Saxon family on better land? Who can tell?

North-east of the town of Ulverston, on the summit of Hoad Hill, (a place-name which may include the altered word haugr, a Viking burial mound), high above the straight line of the old canal, a Victorian monument dominates the town. It looks, to all intents and purposes, like a lighthouse; indeed, it is a good copy of the Eddystone light, built by the famous John Smeaton on the notorious Eddystone reef some 14 miles off Plymouth. Smeaton was consulted about its construction, but this Ulverston "light" carries no beam to sweep a darkened sea; it is not warning to shipping, but a hundred-foot tower of local limestone built by public subscription in 1855. There was rather a sly attempt to obtain some money from the government for its construction by suggesting that it *could* be used as a lighthouse, but this idea found no governmental favour, and no money other than by direct subscription was ever forthcoming.

Now a unique building demanding the attention of every stranger entering the town from the east, the tower is perched on a hump of dark grey mudstone; a summit of dour, slate-like brittle rock towering more than 400 feet above the busy A590 trunk road and the sprawling town. It is a startling monument; a tribute to Ulverston's most famous son, Sir John Barrow. In 1764, he was born in a tiny cottage in the hamlet of Dragley Beck (the bizarrely-named old Norse stream of the dragon) on the southern fringe of the modern town. His parents were smallholders and market-gardeners.

Sir John Barrow - "the best Secretary of the Navy since Pepys"

The Barrow family cottage stands there today, but the steeply pitched thatched roof has been replaced by one of slate; the present occupant is engaged in selling sweets to schoolchildren! There are other memorials to the great Sir John, but these are much less parochial, and are a long, long way from this quiet town. One is the bleak and bitter Barrow Point, the windswept and most northerly tip of Alaska; another is Barrow Strait, well beyond the Arctic Circle in northern Canada.

John Barrow was a very bright and determined youth. He developed quickly into a natural teacher and gifted mathematician, and held several important and responsible jobs before he was 20. These included surveyor's assistant, tutor to a boy barely two years younger than himself, and head book-keeper to a firm of Liverpool iron-founders. When the owner of that firm died, Barrow was out of a job. Filled with the spirit of adventure, he shook off city life, and went whaling off Greenland and Spitzbergen, hunting down the huge, ugly, but highly profitable cetacean, the Greenland Right Whale, *Balaena mystecetus*. Today, this species is rare, but in Barrow's day it was plentiful, the favoured 'Right' whale to catch, hence the common name. John Barrow returned home to Ulverston in triumph, bearing with him a giant pair of whale jawbones, which stood outside his parents' cottage doorway for many years, to the amazement and wonder of generations of less adventurous Ulverstonians!

After the whaling trip, the still very young John Barrow taught mathematics at Greenwich, under the watchful but approving eye of Andrew Maskelyne, then the Astronomer Royal. Mathematics, particularly those used in navigation, plus world travel, ships, and the sea, were the loves of Barrow's long life.

At home Barrow was helped from time to time by another mathematical prodigy, a fell farmer named John Gibson. Naturally gifted, Gibson naively imagined that everyone was as able in the subject as he; he worked out many a problem - merely for his own amusement - using nothing but a piece of chalk and the thighs of his rough cloth breeches; while he was involved in any of the hundred and one jobs which had to be performed on a small fell farm! Gibson worked the Hollins fields, high above the churning River Winster; that narrow stream which once divided the two counties of Lancashire and Westmorland. Hollins farm, now a private house, lies on the eastern slope of the fell beyond Gummers How, looking down to the beautiful little hamlet of Bowland Bridge. John Barrow rode here often; he never forgot the brilliant Gibson who helped him so much with problems of mathematics and marine navigation.

The big break for Barrow, however, came when he was appointed tutor to the young Tom Staunton. This lad was a brilliant linguist, even at 12 years of age, one of the languages known to him was Mandarin (still the official language of mainland China). John Barrow, unable to resist the challenge of his new pupil, was soon speaking and writing the same language with considerable fluency. It was to stand him in good stead. He became the Comptroller of the household of Lord McCartney, a job which took him first to South Africa, and then, later on, to China. Barrow, ever a shrewd observer, wrote brilliantly of his travels, which soon attracted the attention of a British Government always very much concerned with expanding and improving international influence and trade.

Barrow was given the job of Second Secretary to the Admiralty; while another astute Cumbrian, Sir James Graham, was appointed First Sea Lord, and from the beginning, these two men worked well together. Between them, they disposed of much of the cobwebbed bureaucracy then existing in the corridors of power; together, they were a hearty gale which blew through the dusty corridors of the Admiralty. It was a breeze doubly welcome at a time when England was fighting for her very life in the long struggle of the Napoleonic Wars, and in which the Royal Navy was to play such a vital part.

It might be said that the efforts of Barrow, described in his time, and long afterwards as the 'best Secretary of the Navy since Pepys', and his colleague, Sir James Graham, went a long way to assure final victory over Napoleon, and left Britain as the greatest sea-power in the world.

John Barrow was involved, indirectly, in the scandalous affair of the *Bounty* mutiny. He was a close friend of the principal mutineer's family, the Christians, of West Cumberland, and known to the Heywoods, who also had a son involved. Fletcher Christian, the ringleader, was not the oppressed and bullied officer so often described in various accounts of the mutiny. His captain, William Bligh, a brilliant but volatile navigator and seaman, has had an undeservedly bad press over the years. The powerful friends of the Christians and the Heywoods, which included Sir John Barrow, made it very difficult for a blunt and straightforward man like Bligh to escape censure for his part in the sordid affair. Nevertheless, Sir John's account of the mutiny is still regarded as a classic account of the occasion.

After the long and bruising war, and the final defeat and exile of Napoleon on the lonely island of St. Helena (which was the place chosen by Barrow for the defeated Emperor), the British Navy found itself with a horde of bright young officers (most of whom had missed the war) champing at the bit. Accordingly, amongst other projects, the government promoted an Arctic expedition, commanded by Sir John Franklin. The object was to find a north-west passage from the Atlantic to the Pacific across the top, the northernmost part, of Canada. The officers and men, after enduring terrible hardships in the ice, all perished; a north-west passage was certainly found by that fated expedition, but whether Franklin or his men ever realised it can never be known. The Franklin expedition, men and ships together, vanished for years without leaving a trace.

New evidence recently come to light suggests that the Franklin expedition was doomed to failure from the start. The key to the whole sorry affair is ridiculously simple; it was the first official use of tinned food in bulk, and the tins were sealed by lead solder. The lead solder meant that all crew members suffered from lead poisoning almost from the start. Lead poisoning leads to rapid deterioration of mental and physical faculties; it includes terrible stomach disorders and complete mental derangement. In 1986 when the 140-year-old corpses of two expedition members were discovered by accident uniquely preserved in the ice-bound soil of Arctic permafrost and were examined in detail by a team of pathologists, to their horror, the doctors found that the preserved body tissues, teeth, and hair of the cadavers contained toxic amounts of lead! At the time of the Franklin expedition when no one was aware of the danger contained in those soldered tins the loss of two complete ships' crews was completely baffling; particularly when the well-found expedition included men with expert knowledge of similar extreme conditions gained in recent voyages to the Arctic or Antarctica.

John Barrow, so closely connected with the expedition agonised over the disappearance of Sir John and his crew, and it is this affair which is remembered by suitable memorials placed inside the Hoad monument. These include the names of several men involved in the expedition, or prominent in the search for it afterwards. Besides Franklin, the leader, his fellow commander Crozier is remembered. Crozier had been with a previous expedition to Antarctica; the ships being the *Erebus* and *Terror*, two vessels which gave their names to the pair of giant volcanoes then discovered in Victoria Land, on that far southern continent. Fitzjames is also remembered; he sailed with Franklin on that last Arctic expedition and perished with him. Bellot, yet another of these gallant seamen, with old scores apparently forgotten (for he was on loan from the French Navy!) sailed with the searchers at the direct request of Lady Franklin. The surgeon-naturalist Kane, an American, is also present on the Hoad monument list. He made two voyages seeking the lost expedition. The last, in 1854, ended in disaster, when Kane had to abandon his ship, the *Advance*, which had frozen in the pack-ice and was being crushed by it. This gallant American finally struggled to safety across miles of sea-ice to Upernavik, then a Danish settlement on the bleak west coast of Greenland. Altogether, 30 searches for the lost Franklin expedition were mounted over a period of 12 years. Its true fate was realised only when a ship's log was discovered recently, hidden under a cairn of stones on an icy, desolate, Arctic shore, close by the graves of the two seamen, dead from lead poisoning.

There is a subtle reminder of John Barrow's ships - the 'wooden walls of England' of Nelson's and Barrow's time - in the shape of the hill below the Hoad monument. The steep south-western face slides down to the busy trunk road, the A590, this slope, in outline, resembling the slant of the tumblehome, the spreading sides of ships so familiar to Sir John.

Immediately beyond the road below Ulverston Canal appears as a broad and shining stretch of water reaching directly seaward, as straight as an arrow, for more than a mile. Designed by the famous Rennie, architect of London Bridge, the first turf of this canal was cut with due musical ceremony in September, 1793. When completed, two years later, in 1795, and indeed for a long time afterwards, Ulverstonians of the day could truthfully boast that their canal was 'the shortest, widest, deepest and straightest canal in the whole world'! Until the arrival of the Furness

Railway in 1855, which spelt the death of the canal, this neatly engineered stretch of water brought huge benefits to the developing town.

As early as 1774, more than 20 years before the opening of Ulverston Canal, there was a massive export trade in iron ore from the mines of Low Furness to various parts of Britain and the Continent. Most went by sea, for generally the roads in the north were deplorable. Some went from Hammarbank, on the south Ulverston shore, close by the canal's former entrance. The quayside, and some of the buildings used in this early pre-canal trade are still there. The building of the canal increased and aided this traffic and this and other businesses along the canal side, were busy from the start. A huge coastal and developing international trade sprang up at the port of Ulverston - another creek port of Lancaster - almost immediately. Tons of high grade copper ore came here from the Coniston mines, ferried down the lake to Nibthwaite and carried on from there by cumbrous horse and cart. Copper ore came in all shades and colours; bright green malachite (used as eye-shadow thousands of years earlier by Cleopatra!) vied in beauty with brilliant blue azurite, the dark purple bornite and the gold-like glitter of copper pyrites. So much of this last-named material was carried over the narrow country roads from Nibthwaite to Ulverston town that tiny grains of it, dropped, or blown by the wind from the carts, made many a mile of that highway sparkle like gold in the sunshine.

A much more hazardous material, gunpowder, came here from works at Low Wood, Haverthwaite, or from Elterwater, in the mouth of Great Langdale. Both the ship being loaded and workers on or about it were kept in fearful isolation on the long canal side until the precarious cargo was safely aboard and the hazardous work complete. Haematite, the high grade Furness ore from the many local mines, was a constant cargo. So were roofing slates, brought from the Kirkby Quarries over to the north-west along a specially-built moorland 'slate road'. This track still exists, but now, it is nothing more than a delightful ribbon of peat, trampled heather, and sheep-clipped grass over wild and lonely moorland; a place where, amongst other rarities, in summer, one may glimpse that delightful little falcon, the merlin, hunting 'titlarks' - meadow pipits, the cheerful, chirruping sparrows of the fells.

Another rock exported was limestone; either as steel-hard, shaped building blocks, or broken rubble for road hardcore. Some went as slaked lime, a putty-like substance, which mixed with ground sand and fine ashes, made the grey mortar still found in so many old buildings of the Lancashire connurbations. Lime powder for field fertilizer, or perhaps more raw material of plaster, was packed into the ships' holds. So were thousands of wooden cask hoops, made in local home workshops, together with hundreds of spelk baskets used for carrying anything from ships' coal to field potatoes. Birch besoms, fencing posts, cotton goods, and local pig iron and other iron goods ranging from flat-irons to spades and shovels are all in the list of exports. The import trade was just as varied, ranging from Welsh and Lancashire cheeses, Cheshire salt (and more cheese!), glass and pottery, to wines and molasses; from Jamaican rum and sugar to Baltic and North American timber, from fashionable London furniture to costly mirrors, carpets or fabrics for the rising numbers of *nouveaux riches* thriving on the canal trade and the opening up of Ulverston to a bigger world.

The exported pig iron was made at Newland, a hamlet immediately east of Ulverston and almost under the long shadow of Hoad Hill. The fuel used here was charcoal, made with much labour and expertise in the coppiced woods of South Lakeland. The original charcoal iron furnace is still in Newland today; so are the labelled charcoal stores, and the tracks to the furnace bearing dark red traces of haematite from the huge heaps of that ore once stored here. A tiny spade forge, once water-powered from an upland, trout-rich tarn, stands forlornly on the edge of Kirkby Moor, on the other side of Ulverston, to the north. From the old building, sickles, spades and other agricultural tools went down to the canal and into the waiting ships. More of the same came from a similar forge on Lowick Green, along the Crake Valley towards Coniston Water. It too, exists; greatly altered and unrecognisable, it is now a private house.

For more than half a century, the canal water was often crowded with shipping, quite a lot of it built in one of the three Ulverston shipyards on or near the canal; vessels like the small, 16-gun *Hope* for example, launched for the West India Trade, which was often a euphemism for involvement in slavery. Or the 20-gun *Argo*, making her mark on the profitable tobacco trade of West Virginia. The biggest ship of all was the 800-ton *Ulverston*, built with too broad a beam even for this wide canal, and therefore made on a slipway on the south Ulverston foreshore. Many of these Ulverston ships were in the coastal trade about Britain and the Continent; others went to America, or the West Indies, or were involved with the timber trade as far afield as Scandinavia and Russia, as well as the Baltic ports. Some Ulverston ships were captured by French privateers during the Napoleonic Wars, with cargo, ship, and usually, master, all put up for ransom. *Annie McLester*, the last ship of all to be built at Ulverston, was sunk by the gun of a German U-boat during the Great War!

With so much shipping to hand, industry flourished on the banks of the canal. There were anchor and chain works, foundries, warehouses, a paper

Plumpton viaduct, 1855, caused the silting and closure of the Ulverston Canal

mill, sail loft, rope works, block and tackle manufacturers, timber yards and many more establishments on or close by this very busy stretch of water. Ulverston, for well over half a century, was thus a flourishing port as well as busy market town and commercial centre of Low Furness.

Today, blocked off from the sea by a concrete dam, Ulverston Canal can no longer hold or cater for any shipping. The changing, erratic course of the River Leven, plus the building in the 1850's of the Plumpton railway viaduct, which crosses the estuary upstream, caused massive silting in the natural channel leading from sea to canal entrance. By supreme irony much of the ironwork for the Plumpton viaduct of the canal's premier rival, the Furness Railway, was made at one of the canal-side foundries! By more modern irony, the Plumpton viaduct is now under threat, with a suggested £2,000,000 needed to repair and maintain it; a sum which may well put the already repeatedly threatened Carnforth/Barrow railway line in serious jeopardy.

By the mid-1850s, Ulverston Canal was done, outpaced by the railway. Odd vessels continued to use it from time to time, but the last steamer to visit was a coal-burning coaster way back in 1916. The very last ship of all to use the canal was the *Nahula*, formerly the *Mollie*, a fine 30-foot yacht, which left the canal in 1946. Still in existence at the time of writing, and formerly berthed at Glasson Dock, across the Bay, the *Nahula* has been sold again and gone elsewhere.

All the proud Ulverston ships are gone; none of any kind has sailed the smooth canal water for more than 40 years. The busy workmen, the bustle of thriving industry, are all missing from the canal-side, the well-stocked warehouses either pulled down long ago or now altered out of all recognition. These days, the long towpath is nothing more than a pleasant walkway, a narrow road and pleasant venue in which to take a quiet stroll, or to exercise the dog. It is a place for patient anglers, or for those who merely like to be on or near the water. Rennie's former busy commercial centre is quiet; cleaned, tidied and sanitised along its whole length; permanently sealed off from the sea, wooden lock-gates rotted away years ago, replaced by steel and concrete. The canal water has a new use; as coolant, after which the water is recycled by the giant Glaxo chemical complex alongside the right bank. Busy making penicillin, streptomycin and other important antibiotics, it is a replacement of the old North Lonsdale ironworks, whose blast furnaces and tall, reeking chimneys once on the same site were a familiar pattern on the Ulverston skyline.

Dalton, five miles to the west of Ulverston was once a bitter rival. Though a market of old, Ulverston did not replace Dalton as the commercial and administration centre of Low Furness until after the dissolution of Furness Abbey in 1537. Bereft of the influence of mighty Furness Abbey, Dalton went quickly into commercial decline, leaving very few reminders of its former glory.

One visible remnant of Dalton's former power is the small, near-square 'Castle', a 14th century tower of limestone and sandstone in the old market square. Looking down the long avenue of busy Market Street, the principal thoroughfare, often overcrowded with traffic, the Dalton 'Castle' is nothing more than a pele tower; one of dozens erected in the spate of building which followed the Scots incursions. It was built to shelter the local people against this 'Scots Plague', which restarted violently in 1314 after two centuries of comparative quiet in Furness. In that year, the inept Edward II and his massive army were routed at Bannockburn by the determined forces of Robert the Bruce. Which meant that the whole Border Country, and much of England immediately south of it, at least as far as Preston, was left wide open to the Scots raiders. Dalton suffered badly, as the record shows:

> 'A.D. 1316: The Scots, renewing their hostilities a second time, plundered Cumberland, Westmorland, Tynedale, Swaledale, Kendale, the Monastery of Furness and Furness Fells, and returned in triumph to Scotland with great spoil. They also burnt many villages in their fury, whilst those resisting were either taken prisoner or perished by the sword ...'.

The 'Great Raid' of 1322, when Bruce came south again, but this time with thousands of men, also meant wholesale devastation of parts of Furness. Dalton was burned to the ground, and such was the destruction that for years afterwards much of the land lay waste. The peasants formerly looking after the land and the cattle and sheep on it had mostly vanished. Many men and women were prisoners of the Scots, dead in the skirmishes, or fled elsewhere. For as chronicled in the State Papers of the time:

> '...In the year of Grace, 1322, the Scots came into England through the midst of Furness and the county of Lancaster, laying waste on all sides, and without damage to themselves, collecting an immense booty of gold and silver, animals, church ornaments, bedding, linen etc., taking away cartloads of all the goods of the country at their pleasure ...'.

Furness Abbey escaped destruction by paying Bruce a huge ransom; 'protection money' of £10,000, which, in 1322, was an immense sum. There is a simple but very grim record of the event in yet another account of the marauders from beyond the Border. A huge army of Scots, with Bruce at their head, came down the west coastal plain ...

> 'laying waste Copeland (much of modern-day West Cumbria) ... and so beyond the Sands of Duddon to Furness; but the Abbot of Furness went to meet him and paid ransom for the district of Furness that it should not be again burnt or plundered, and took him to Furness Abbey. This, notwithstanding, the Scots set fire to various places and lifted spoil ...'.

Is it any wonder that even today, some of the older Daltonians mutter that 'Nowt good ever comes round Black Combe'? This old saying is in obvious memory of those 14th century Scots invasions, for there is no doubt that Bruce's invasion was by way of the west coast and by crossing the Duddon estuary - the 'Duddon Sands' of the original record - into Furness.

More than 300 years after this, but soon after the trauma of the Dissolution of the Monasteries (here, with the Abbey of Furness, it happened in 1537), Dalton sank in importance as Ulverston began to rise. From then on, Ulverston seemed to thrive; today, even with the loss of the canal and its trade, without the status and use of port facilities, the town is a thriving commercial and agricultural centre. Every Thursday, this being market day at Ulverston, the pubs remain open all day, mostly from 11.00 a.m. to 11.00 p.m. This welcome custom, granted by special charter years before the present loosening of the licensing laws, is fiercely defended, principally by a host of thirsty fell farmers as well as Ulverston townsfolk!

Due west of Hoad monument on its high and rocky hill, but tucked well down below it, the ancient parish church of Ulverston stands in its own little-used and peaceful graveyard. Dedicated to St. Mary, traditionally founded in 1111 A.D., it is known to Ulverstonians as the 'Church of the Four Ones'. Over the centuries, much of the fabric has been altered, and a lot added to it since those very early days. Even so, a surprising amount of original work remains. The main doorway is pure Norman; an arch of typical dogtooth pattern in yellowing sandstone, fortunately sheltered from the weather by a more modern porch. The square tower replaces one which fell down centuries ago during a violent thunderstorm. Half-way up this pile of weathered stones, a reminder and relic of the former tower destroyed by tempest, is an eroded, exfoliated sandstone tablet. Badly worn, the inscription once incised deeply into the brown-red rock has long been worn away. Fortunately for the historian, it was carefully written down before it finally disappeared. It reads as follows, the translation, for ease of understanding, being placed opposite, line by line:

"PRAY FOR THE SOWLE	PRAY FOR THE SOUL
OF WILLm DOBSON GEN	OF WILLIAM DOBSON, GENTLEMAN
VSHR TO QUEN ELH WCH	USHER TO QUEEN ELIZABETH WHICH(!)
GAVE UNTO THIS WORKE	GAVE UNTO THIS WORK ..."

Unfortunately, the amount given by Sir William was not recorded before erosion destroyed that part of the original inscription.

The curious "QUEN ELH" of the carving was not Good Queen Bess, Elizabeth I, but one of our forgotten queens, Elizabeth Woodville, daughter of the Yorkist Edward IV, who was brother to that bold, bad Duke of Gloucester who later became Richard III.

With regards to the re-building of the Ulverston church tower, it would seem that Elizabeth Woodville had promised to furnish the necessary money. However, it also appears that she found the cost too high (or was denied it by her notoriously parsimonious husband?). Her donation paid for the work on the tower up the level of the inscription, and Sir William, member of a local family risen to high court rank, came to her aid and paid for the rest of the work built above the sandstone tablet.

Inside the church, there is a remarkable Elizabethan brass to the local Dodding family, but, at first glance, pride of place for all things old must go to the marvellous sarcophagus topped by a recumbent figure in full and rich Elizabethan dress. This is the memorial to William Sandys (pronounced Sands), son of Sir William Sandys, the King's Receiver (agent) immediately after the dissolution of Furness Abbey. Son William, as will be described in more detail later, was murdered by his own tenants on the front lawn of Conishead Priory, a couple of miles to the south of the town. This happened in 1558; his body was thrown into the sea, and never recovered. Rumour says that his memorial, this proud church effigy, despite its apparent antiquity, is neither carved from expensive alabaster, which it seems, or of work older than early Victorian. It was erected by the powerful and influential Braddylls, who were the tenants of Conishead Priory early in the 19th century before being bankrupted out of existence there.

The 'Church of the Four Ones', however, was not always as peaceful as it appears today. There was tremendous uproar inside it one day in 1658, when George Fox appeared in this 'steeplehouse', as he called all churches, despite the obvious fact that Ulverston parish church had a tower and not a spire. Fox, the founder of the Quaker movement, had challenged the philosophy of the resident parish priest, a staunch Presbyterian minister called Lampitt, and continued to argue with him while being ejected violently from the church. Once outside, Fox was set upon once again by more enraged parishioners, and badly beaten. The event is carefully recorded in Fox's journal:

> 'I went near to the priest Lampitt, who was blustering on in his preaching ... John Sawrey, the Justice ... said that if I would speak according to the Scriptures, I should speak ... then he said I should not speak ... the people were quiet, and heard me gladly till this Justice Sawrey ... the first stirrer-up of cruel persecution in the North ... incensed them against me, and set them on to hale, beat, and bruise me ... on a sudden, the people were in a rage, and fell upon me in the steeple-house ... knocked me down ... and trampled upon me ... and put me out of town ...'.

This sickening incident 'convinc'd' Margaret Fell, wife of Judge Fell, of Swarthmoor, who was at the service - 'convinc'd' was the Quaker way of saying she took up their religion - and brought her into the gentle Quaker fold for the rest of her long life.

Like so many old parish churches, St. Mary's of Ulverston has some very interesting tombstones within the churchyard. Perhaps the most unusual of all is a small, green-algaed cube of freestone dedicated to the widow of a sea captain killed in action more than two hundred years ago. His widow was Isobel, and he was John McCartney, captain of the *Princess Amelia,* a ship of the line, an 80-gun third-rater, who met his death on her quarterdeck on the 5th August, 1751, during the Battle of the Doggers Bank. He died fighting against an escorted Dutch convoy in an event regarded by many at the time as no more than a skirmish, but one which left more than 400 men dead and wounded on each side. Only one ship flying the Dutch flag was sunk in the long engagement. In the same sea battle was Lieutenant Bligh, later to command the *Bounty*. At Doggers Bank, Bligh was the commander of *La Belle Poule*, a nippy little frigate carrying messages and transmitting flag signals during the battle; she had been captured years earlier from the French, as her name suggests. Poor John McCartney was killed early in the Doggers Bank engagement; his widow, Isobel, never recovered from the shock of his death. She died some eighteen months later, leaving five children, and it was they who put up this simple memorial to Isobel and her husband in Ulverston churchyard.

To the south of the town, away from the old church, and built a short time after the death of the gallant captain, Prince Street, one of the main thoroughfares is prim and Georgian. Several houses there are built in similar classical style, and one, the former office of the Ministry of Agriculture and Fisheries, bears a pair of unusual trees in the front garden. These are ginkgos, the Chinese maidenhair trees; each a living fossil of very long ancestry. The fan-shaped leaves of this strange tree, identical with the modern species, have been found in chalk deposits of the Cretaceous era, some 140 million years old. Around Ulverston there are several specimens of this rather rare tree, which was first brought back to this country as a garden novelty in 1758. It has never been found growing wild in its native China. The Ulverston imports came from cultivated specimens growing in Chekiang Province, an eastern coastal province of that vast country.

Leading almost due north, away from the main road through the town, is Soutergate, which climbs steeply towards the distant moors between rows of 18th and early 19th century houses. The name Soutergate, which is undoubtedly from the old Norse tongue, means 'the

The sign of the Bugle Horn on this house in Soutergate indicates an old coaching inn of that name

Soutergate - does it really mean Shoemaker Street, or should it be Soutargate, meaning Sheep Street?

street of the shoemakers', but I wonder if there is another and possibly more correct interpretation? Certainly there were lots of different trades carried on in this ancient street, and these included blacksmiths, pub-keepers, bakers and undoubtedly shoemakers amongst many others. The trumpet-like carving on the front wall of one tall old house betrays an ancient coaching inn of that proud name, the *Bugle Horn;* a relic of the days when the stage-coaches came and went to and from old Cumberland by this steep descent into the town. Yet dare I suggest that Soutergate should really be spelt Soutargate? That one letter difference in the spelling makes all the difference, for though *souter* means shoemaker, the homonym, *soutar*, means, in old Icelandic dialect, a sheep. Souter - or Soutar-gate leads down directly from the rough grazing of the moorland beyond the town; it was (and still is) used by shepherds and flockmasters in that area to bring their stock to market, though usually by vehicle these days rather than on foot. So is it truly Souter? Or should it be Soutar? The argument continues!

Beyond Ulverston railway station, which is a charming mid-Victorian piece of architecture fiercely defended against alteration by Ulverstonians, a grassy path leads past the Catholic junior school. It makes a delightful walk, for after a few yards, it dips down to the chattering shallows of a swift-

Swarthmoor Hall, the house of Margaret Fell who married George Fox

running beck, under the shadow of some tall and elegant trees. The track continues over the stream by an old packhorse bridge, and heads uphill after crossing marshy ground which in late spring is glorious with buttercup and marsh marigold, later with blue forget-me-not. Within a few more yards, the path leads by the sturdy grey walls of Swarthmoor Hall, a lovely old building which is part Elizabethan, part Jacobean, set in gentle green meadowland.

As the name suggests, this was moorland long before the Enclosure Acts of the 17th, 18th and 19th centuries enclosed a lot of such common land. Though these various Acts improved the national organisation and practice of agriculture tremendously and brought huge new areas under cultivation, they also deprived many poor folk, the poverty-stricken 'cottars', or cottagers, of the last free grazing for sheep, cows and geese. Originally, then, the Hall was on the edge of a windswept *Swarth* moor, which means the Black moor. By a strange and bizarre coincidence, the captain of the forces bound for defeat and death at Stoke Field in June, 1487 - the very last battle of the Wars of the Roses - camped here overnight with some 8,000 men. He was a German mercenary, Captain Schwarz - but the moor had been named long before his day!

Swarthmoor Hall is now known the world over as one of the most important of all Quaker centres. It was the home of Judge Fell and his wife Margaret who had been converted to Quakerism on observing the treatment of George Fox in the Parish Church. Later on, both before and after Margaret being widowed, it was the regular meeting place of the Quakers. Eventually, it became the home of their leader, George Fox, for Margaret married old 'Leather britches' himself.

The Hall still holds some of their possession, such as the four-poster bed in which they slept. Today, it is left undisturbed, but complete with original 17th century blankets and bedding, with a carpet of similar age - in remarkable condition - on the bedroom floor alongside. The colours are surprisingly bright and clear, even after more than 300 years of existence! The bed is kept in the huge attic, directly under the timbered roof. In one corner is a travelling bag which belonged to Fox, and his sea-chest, used when he went to America; indeed, in this lovely old house, there are many reminders of the 17th century and the industrious Quakers.

The Hall today is a peaceful, gentle place, as befits Quaker ideals, but it must be remembered that it was not always so. During the Civil War, in 1643, Roundhead troops were billeted here briefly before being involved in the Battle of Lindal; a brief skirmish on the heights above Dalton some three miles west of the Hall. It was a short and nasty affair, in which 12 men were killed. The Royalists, a band of badly trained, ill-armed troops broke away quickly and ran for home. Home for most of them was south Cumberland, across the wide and treacherous Duddon Sands. An old tradition insists that some 200 of these men were caught by the incoming tide, and drowned. Yet I can find no record of this tragedy, nor does any parish register confirm it. If 200 men were drowned, where were they buried? The sea cannot have taken all of them! I can find nothing, but there is another decidedly sour note in the aftermath of this short battle. It is that the supposedly puritanical and deeply religious Roundheads went down after the battle into Dalton and behaved in a most ungodly and un-Christian fashion by a shocking display of vandalism, looting, drinking and generally behaviour which terrified the helpless and harmless occupants of the old town.

There is another and even darker side to these far-off times, for as with all early Dissenters (as people who sought simpler forms of worship were called), the Quakers were subjected to great and continuous persecution for many years. Both Margaret and George spend much time in prison. Even so, the Quaker movement flourished, particularly in the North, where dissension with the church was rife.

Though not numerically strong today, the local Quakers still use the Meeting House built in 1688, not far from Swarthmoor Hall. Several more were built, and some remain, in various parts of Cumbria, and most are worth a visit. The Swarthmoor Meeting House is full of interest, if only for the fact that George Fox himself bought the property in 1687 for the sum of £72 from two of Judge Fell's daughters. He gave it to the Friends, and wrote that 'I offer and give up freely to the Lord, for ever, and for the service of his sons and daughters and servants called Quakers, the house and houses, barn, kiln, stable, and all the land, with the garden and orchard, being about 3 acres of Land more or less ... called Pettis at Swarthmore ...'. At the same time, Fox suggested that '... I would have the meeting place large, for truth may increase ...'. He also asked that the Ulverston Friends '... were not to be at a farthing charge, but iff friends of ye meetinge or therways will come with there carts and help to fetch stone, lyme, wood, sand or slate: I shall take yt kindely ...'. Though the porch lintel of the Meeting House is inscribed 'EX DONO: G.F. 1688', it was not used regularly until 1690, as Fox insisted that 'ffriends are not to meet in it soe longe as ffriends can meet at Swarthmore Hall ...'. The name of the site is fascinating; "Pettis" is a Furnessian rendering of the surname Petty, from the old Norman-French 'petit', meaning a small man. As a surname, Petty, a direct derivation, is known from the early days of Furness Abbey, in the first half of the 12th century. In that form, or as Pettit, more than two dozen people are listed in the current telephone directory for the Furness and North Lonsdale areas.

Across the broad green fields, the former moorland over to the north-west, beyond the houses of Swarthmoor and across the main A590 trunk road leading to Dalton and Barrow, is the village of Pennington. Tucked into a tiny valley, dominated by a sturdy grey church on its own hill, this is yet another Low Furness settlement of ancient lineage. The name betrays it; Pennington is the *inga-tun,* or large, village-size settlement of the Saxon family called Penn, or perhaps Pennings. It is also associated with pre-history, for by the quiet stream, which once worked the village corn mill, there is a large mound. This is Ellabarrow, said by the place-name specialists to mean 'barrow, or hand-made hummock, or mound, with alder trees'. Yet, according to the old local tale, this is nonsense! Here, it says, is the grave-mound where sleeps King Ella of the Golden Sword, ready to awaken, like King Arthur, whenever England has need of him! I wonder if the golden sword is a dim and distant folk memory of gleaming Bronze Age weapons? Could the story be *THAT* old? It is quite likely that Ellabarrow is the grave of a Bronze Age chieftain of perhaps four thousand years ago, but the mound-site has never been excavated - at least not officially! It is a striking coincidence, however, that close by is a cottage called Conygerhurst, which means King's mound. It is also a fact that when the present cottage foundations were being dug, several bronze Age artefacts were indeed recovered from a small barrow there.

A more obvious historical treasure, however, is kept inside the church. This is a tympanum, a stone lintel for some vanished church once standing here, perhaps on the modern site. The old lintel, removed from a barn wall earlier this century, is inscribed in the strange and spidery lines of Norse runes, the angular Viking alphabet called the *furthark* after the name of its first seven letters. Dated to about the last quarter of the 12th century, which seems to fall in line with other clues and records, the lintel inscription reads KML· SETE THES KIRK HUBIRT MASUM UAN M, which has been translated as 'Gamel founded this church. Hubert the mason built it ...'. It may betray a mixture of races and tongues, for Hubert as a name shows strong Norman influence, while the use of runes suggest that the old Norse language was still being spoken and read in this districts at that time, a full century after the Norman Conquest. It is quite likely, for the old Cumbrian dialect - almost a sub-language, but now spoken by fewer and fewer people, is rich with words straight from the old Norse tongue. A minor but perhaps important other indicator is that many of the mason marks in Furness Abbey, particularly those on 12th and 13th century pillars and other masonry, are straight copies of some of the letters from the same Norse alphabet!

The Gamel of the rune-inscriptions is almost certainly Gamel de Pennington, 12th century Norman overlord of the Pennington district. A farm at the edge of the moor may be named after him; this is Gamswell, which means Gamel's spring, or draw-well. At Castle Hill Farm high above the village towards Kirkby Moor there are the battered remnants of a still-recognisable Norman motte and bailey where he may also have lived, though there is argument about it. Others suggest it was a Saxon *burgh* (a stronghold built long before the Normans arrived) first occupied by the chieftain of the Penn family, as a turf and timber stronghold high above his family's wattle and daub *ingatun*, or village.

The dedication of the first church recorded here was to St. Leonard, the patron saint of lepers (and prisoners!). There is also the legend of a *spital* in the vicinity, a type of medieval hospital also often associated with lepers. The evidence of this is the name Loppergarth, a section of the modern village, which means the garden, or small-holding, of the lepers. Less kindly folk point out it might equally well be a derivation of *loupar-garth*. A *loupar* was literal old Norse for a leaper - but actually meaning, in Viking slang, a fly-boy, a trickster, a shady dealer!

Perhaps the best Norman relic of all in the Ulverston area is the former

Priory of Conishead, almost on the shore of Morecambe Bay. It was founded in the early 12th century as a religious house, possibly first as a hospital, by the Augustinian Order. Like all such establishments, it was totally destroyed - economically if not physically - by the agents of Henry VIII in 1536, a year before Furness Abbey's breakdown. The proud fabric damaged, the statues torn down or defaced, the gold and silver put in the king's hands, and most other possessions scattered far and wide, the magnificent Priory ended up in the hands of a greedy local squire, an entrepreneur who acted as the Royal Agent while pocketing much profit from the demise of this lovely religious house.

Beyond the Priory, far out on the treacherous sands of the Bay is Chapel Island. Bush-shrouded, in outline it is rather like a squat submarine under way with little more than the conning tower showing. It bears the stark gable end of a tumbled chapel, which is a fake; erected by the Braddylls of the Priory during the early Victorian craze for antiquities, even if such antiquities were often obvious and blatant 'follies'. The Braddyll folly, however, does have some authenticity. It is built on the remains of an older chapel, a stone cell probably of the 13th century. Here, the monks said prayers for the safety of travellers crossing the dangerous sands. The tiny original building became a haven for those escaping the rushing tides, which have drowned so many incautious travellers over the centuries. Men like the 13th century Lord of Aldingham, who crossed the sands towards Conishead after dining with the Prior of Cartmel. Obviously, he had dined well, but not wisely, for the old record states that:

> 'On Coena Domina, the Supper of Our Lord, to wit, the day of St. Benedict, Abbot, Thursday, March 21st, 1269, Sir Michael de Furness was drowned on Leven Sands ... he had dined with the Prior of Cartmel, and when at the time intoxicated ... he was attempting to cross with his family to his manor of Aldingham, on the other side of the Leven, he only perished, the others escaping with difficulty, nor was he ever found ...'.

Conishead Priory, though much altered over the years, and after many trials and tribulation, has come full circle. Surprisingly, today it is the home of more monks; but these are the gentle followers of the great Lord Buddha, treading yet another path of Enlightenment, meeting other gods in a language strange to most western ears. These gentle folk, and their industrious followers, by dint of much faith and even more hard work, are gradually restoring the Priory to much of its former architectural glory. Visitors of any race, colour, or religious persuasion, are made welcome.

So Conishead once again has the smell of incense, and a monastic silence and tranquillity reigns over much of the building. There is the quiet chant and murmur of religious prayers. Is it not strange? To find monks once more living in this part of modern Cumbria after a break of more than 450 years? Still by the shore of Morecambe Bay, and within the stout fabric of what was once a medieval Augustinian Priory?

4: South Front

THE MAIN ROAD from Ulverston to the shores of Morecambe Bay runs almost due south from the town. It passes the Gothic spires of Conishead Priory, which is worthy of even more attention.

Though still bearing traces of an ancient religious house, much of the original Priory fabric has been replaced by the stonework of a huge mansion (the result of early Victorian re-building) built at enormous cost, but continuing on a site which is at least 850 years old. In its time, the Priory has been home to black-robed Augustinian monks, an Elizabethan entrepreneur murdered here on his own front lawn, an Anglo-Swiss iron-ore baron, a convalescent home to coal and lead miners, wounded servicemen of World War II, and finally, today, a Buddhist monastery.

Conishead Priory was founded as a hospital in the 12th century during the reign of Henry II. There is no clear date of its foundation, but a deed of 1167 may hold the answer. A later deed, of 1180, from William Lancaster, Baron of Kendal, gave the Priory all Conishead, the church at Ulverston, and 40 acres of its fields, a salt works, a corn mill, and rights of turbary (cutting peat for fuel). Permission by the same deed for cattle pasturage, pannage (allowing pigs to grub for acorns in the woods) and timber-taking in the Baron's Furness woodland was also given.

At Conishead, almost on the shore of Morecambe Bay, the dedicated monks may have found the peace, devotion both to God and less fortunate humans, and the comparative isolation demanded by their austere Order. The Conishead Augustinians, as with so many religious houses, took on what the late Victorian colonial administrators described as 'The white man's burden'. They helped the sick, the poor, and the aged. They dealt out hospitality as did other religious houses; but theirs was particularly important at this remote spot, for it involved the care of travellers crossing the treacherous expanse of Morecambe Bay between the tides. So concerned were these good men, that they built the chapel on Chapel Island, then called Harlesyde, far out on the sands of the Bay between the Cartmel and Furness peninsulas.

Colonel Braddyll, builder of the Chapel Island folly, was also so keen an antiquarian that he employed a servant to live as 'hermit' in a specially built 'natural' cell within the Priory grounds, but only on the assurance that to add authenticity, the 'hermit' would never cut either his nails or hair! The

Conishead Priory; the rebuilding bankrupted the owner, Col. Bradyll

same Colonel rebuilt the Priory, and bankrupted himself and family in doing so in the middle of the 19th century. The building costs went up to £140,000, and this, together with failure in several coal mining ventures, left him a ruined man. Amongst other expensive items, special building stone for the new Priory had been imported by ship from a quarry at Overton, across the Bay, near Lancaster.

The Elizabethan murdered there, and remembered by a carved (but empty!) tomb in Ulverston Parish Church, was William Sandys, son of the first Receiver of Furness, mentioned in Chapter 2 but worthy of a fuller tale. The Receiver was a Crown Agent, controlling the Furness Abbey and Conishead Priory estates after both of these had been broken up by Henry VIII in the nationwide Dissolution of the Monasteries of 1536 and 1537. Neither Sandys, father or son, was ever popular, for both were greedy entrepreneurs and bad landlords. Local bad feeling towards the young Sandys is revealed by old records: 'William Bardseye bore malice against him for concealing a piece of land from the Queen'. John Preston, who was William Sandys' uncle, threatened to have him put in the stocks at Dalton. John Richardson, of Dalton 'made a fray upon Sandy's servant at Roose milne (corn mill) ... and cut of (off) towe (two) of the thumbs of the servantes of the said William Sandys ...'! Many other local people appear to have held grudges against the two Sandys. So it is not altogether surprising that on the

10th September, 1558, when the younger William confronted his enraged and long-suffering tenants on his front lawn of Conishead (which he had bought from the Crown, to the envy and disturbance of the local people), that he was promptly 'very riotously and wylfully murdered'. He certainly needed a course of what today would be called man-management; instead of listening to the tenants' complaints, he reached into his Bible, and contemptuously threw out the following phrase, from the Book of Kings, to the angry mob: 'Whereas my father did lade you with an heavy yoke, I will add to your yoke; my father hath chastised you with whips, but I will chastise you with scorpions!'. This from a member of a family which 20 years previously, were little more than poor farmers? It was too much; the proverbial last straw for the angry assembly. Led by Nicholas Bardsey, last in the male line of an old and respected local family, the furious crowd attacked and beat William to death, flinging his corpse into the tide from which it was never recovered. Nicholas was charged, in his absence, with the crime at Lancaster Castle, but apparently neither arrested nor convicted. He exiled himself in Scotland for a while, came back to his native Urswick, and thenceforth, led an apparently blameless life, becoming governor of the village grammar school, founded a year before his death in 1586, two years before the nation's clash with the Spanish Armada. The school still exists, not as a Free Grammar, but a busy and bustling school for village infants.

For a long time, The Priory, as a convalescent home, catered for miners from the north-east. Some came to recover from painful industrial injury sustained in this still most-dangerous of trades. Others hoped to ease the agonies of silicosis, in which lungs are coated with mining dust over a long period, causing laboured, wheezy breathing, much reduced physical activity and eventually, a painful early death. Casualties of World War II convalesced here also; and General of the German S.S. died there (of a heart attack, let me hasten to add!), before once again the post-war Priory returned to treating the miners. The Priory became empty for a while, and there was talk of it being the new University for Cumbria. Finally, the role of the Priory turned full circle and was once more occupied by monks! These fellow religious workers are of an older faith; peaceful Buddhists of the Manjishri Institute, who unlike the sterner Augustinians of so long ago, allow visitors of any faith, or no faith at all, free access to the lovely buildings and beautiful grounds.

Half a mile beyond the Priory, down a wide, tree-lined avenue more like the approach to a stately home than a busy road, the tarmacked surface swings abruptly right. This is the beginning of the coast road, which follows the edge of Morecambe Bay west as far as the village of Rampside, about eight miles away. Much of the route is right beside the shore, protected in places against the onslaught of winter waves by a stout concrete wall. The whole section, whether at low tide or full, is delightful. Pleasing to the eye, rich in natural history, and passing close by places full of historical interest, the coast road is quite a showpiece in Low Furness. It was built in the terrible depression of pre-war years mostly by local job-starved men, and it does them credit.

The first village met is Bardsea, built high above the stony shore on a large rounded hill, one of the many drumlins in the district. Like Conishead, Bardsea has roots deep in history, and some of this may be seen on the ground. A mixture of old and new houses, with some dating back to the 17th century, it was an agricultural settlement probably before the Domesday Book of 1086 was written. In that famous tome, it is recorded as 'Berretseige', which means precisely nothing. As this was probably written down by Norman-French clerks with little knowledge of English, let alone local dialect, the old Bardsea title has been a source of controversy and argument ever since. I find it significant that Berretseige, when spoken aloud, sounds remarkably like Bardsea, voiced as Baird-see in old local dialect.

The tall-spired church, of near-white local limestone, is separate from other buildings. It was built in mid-Victorian times, on a beautiful site overlooking the wide expanse of Morecambe Bay, though there were very troubled beginnings. Colonel Braddyll, of the Priory, was one of the main instigators of the church scheme, but unfortunately, his bankruptcy fell right in the middle of the proceedings. There was argument over ownership of the land set aside for the site, and not enough money to finish the building; but, eventually, the whole problem was solved, and very simply.

The son of another rich and ancient local family, the Pettys, stepped in and paid for the

Bardsea Church, saved by the Petty family when the Bradylls went bankrupt

completion of the church. Being a reverend, he was promptly installed as the first curate! He and his sister are remembered by three stained glass windows, but there is also an object kept in the church which may be a reminder of Bardsea's more distant past. This is a brass alms dish, possibly of 16th or 17th century origin, graphically inscribed in old Dutch, of all languages! The deep-cut inscription reads as follows:

'Wylt Ghy hy Langhellwen too ert Goot ert hoovt zyn gebat vorwar', which translates as 'if thou would'st live long - fear God and keep his commandments'.

No one seems to know whence it came, but there was an older chapel here long before the present church was built. Was the strange brass dish one belonging to the earlier building? Or is it a relic of the old iron-ore trade, when many vessels were beached at low tide on the shore, and men loaded them with the rich haematite carted here from the 18th century mines of Low Furness? Many of these vessels grounding on Bardsea sands were from Liverpool, locally owned, or Welsh, carrying the haematite down to the busy foundries beyond the Dee. Was the church bowl given by a Continental captain? In grateful thanks after a rough voyage, or rescue from the treacherous waters of the Bay?

Bardsea as a place-name, may well be a corruption of 'Barnards-ey' (Bernard's Isle) an old memory of the time when the ground below the village was a sea-washed marsh, and gave the place the illusion of being an island. The first Bardsea settlement by incoming Normans was probably made early in the 12th century, and by the Knights Hospitallers, possibly even as a leper colony of sorts. It never became more than a fishing and farming village, though in the early 18th century it was involved in the Furness iron-ore trade. In 1840, it began to encourage tourists, the Bardsea shore being arrival and departure point for steamers crossing and re-crossing the Bay from and to Fleetwood and Liverpool. The long wooden pier from which the first ships departed has long since gone, but the old sea wall once abutting it remains, by the former mill. Now labelled the 'Old Mill Café', the present buildings were part of a thriving corn mill until the 1920s. The wooden machinery, and the undershot water-wheel, have disappeared. So have the original millstones; a millstone does stand against the wall; this large example is made of granite, but it is merely for show. Granite, even the best, was unsuitable for milling corn, as it breaks away under pressure, spreading quartz and silica grains amongst any flour being milled. This would cause havoc to teeth chewing bread made from any such flour! The Bardsea café wheel came from an Ulverston paper mill, a place demolished

Broughton Square (Photo: Walt Unsworth)

In Cartmel village (Photo: Walt Unsworth)

years ago. The mill pond, barely recognisable under its growth of reed, bulrush and yellow flag, still exists, a weed-choked marsh, at the side of the modern café.

Some three hundred yards west of the café, the coast road turns and sweeps uphill through mature woodland. A mixture of oak, beech, birch and ash, this is Seawood, reputedly a source of timber for the 18th and early 19th century ships of the Royal Navy. It is Crown property, and has been so since that fateful day in 1554, when Mary, Henry VIII's fanatical daughter and wife of Philip of Spain, ordered the execution of the beautiful, accomplished, but usurping Lady Jane Grey, tragic queen of England for 11 days! When Mary succeeded to the Crown she promptly took over Lady Jane's many estates, a tiny part of which included Sea Wood.

This wood of large trees may be as silent as a tomb, or loud with bird song according to the time and season. It is one of the few places in Low Furness where one might find the brimstone, a sulphur-coloured butterfly (in the

Seawood at Bardsea; Crown property gained on the execution of Lady Jane Grey in 1554

male, that is), so often on the wing in early March. The caterpillar may remain dormant all winter in shelter, emerging as the weather warms, to change into the beautiful butterfly, an insect which by its bright yellow colour may be the original butter (coloured) fly! Surprisingly hardy, the brimstone caterpillar feeds heartily on the leaves of alder buckthorn, which, if eaten by human or animal, is a highly dangerous purgative.

Other inhabitants of Seawood include green woodpecker, carrion crow, the inevitable magpie, tree-creeper, tawny owl, and many of the smaller woodland passerines. Of the crows, the jay is hardest to find and watch; so are the cautious woodpigeons, each with a nest so frail that one may see this cushat's round, white eggs by looking up through the bottom of the nesting platform! Mammals found here include wide-eared woodmice, weasel, stoat, hedgehog, and occasionally, sheltering roe deer, hidden in the deepest of thickets. Barn owls visit, hunting the fringes; the busy tits and finches, particularly in winter, work every inch of the branches in search of insect or seed.

Of all the many things found in this wood, the most interesting to me are the black, rounded knoblets of fungi known either as Cramp balls, or, more delightfully, King Alfred's cakes. These grow on the underside of diseased branches of ash, and do not attack living wood. The scientific name is *Daldinia concentrica,* for when the hard, woody fungus is cut in two, the annual, concentric growth rings, as in trees and shrubs, are plain to see. King Alfred's cakes is an obvious name; but why Cramp balls? Supposedly, this fungi if put in the pocket, will prove a great preventative of cramp; or if one is attacked by cramp, it is also supposed to cure it, though how, and why, I have no idea; nor if it really works. For me, it certainly does not!

The talls trees of Seawood make a marvellous shelter from the rains and gales of spring, or those of autumn, with soft leaf-strewn paths a delight underfoot. This is a place in which to meander, to walk with little purpose other than to enjoy the peace and tranquillity of it all. One such path runs along the top of the wood, and by way of large, moss-grown limestone outcrops, emerges once again onto a loop of the coast road. Along it, half a mile away, is the Quaker village of Baycliffe. Here, hidden from the road by a rash of new bungalows, is a charming collection of old, stone-built houses, with thick walls and massive chimneys, some huge and rounded in the unique Westmorland style. The Myers family, living here for generations have a house with such a chimney; indeed, the squat and curious stack gives a nickname to the building of 'Top Hat'! Several village houses retain huge ingle-nooks, each a massive fireplace of the late 17th century; places where hard-working, God-fearing gentle Quakers warmed themselves, or hung mutton and bacon therein, to smoke and dry for winter use, always wondering, in the early days of the movement, where and when the next persecutors would arrive.

Baycliffe became very busy in the middle of the 18th century. Then, as with so many coastal villages and hamlets of Low Furness, the village was engaged in the iron-ore traffic. With few natural harbours, the method was simple. The rich haematite ore was carted to dumps on the shoreline, but clear of the highest tides. It was then loaded by wheelbarrow into the capacious holds of flat-bottomed, broad-beamed 'Flatts', which sat, on even keel, on the sands and mud at low tide. When the tide came in, the ships floated off with the cargo and sailed away; some to Welsh foundries, some to the charcoal iron foundry at the head of the Duddon estuary, just beyond Duddon Bridge; others fed the furnaces of Low Wood, near Haverthwaite, the charcoal iron foundry at Backbarrow, and the small iron works perched above the River Crake at Pennybridge. Baycliffe, even as a small village, became very busy in the iron-ore trade because of two things. First it was close to the sea for easy onward transport of the haematite, and the mines were not far away by reasonable, short roads. Second, almost on the shore was a powerful spring. From this, pure fresh water, needed by every vessel which called here, could be taken on board very easily. This spring has never dried up; it flowed steadily and freely even during the long summer drought of 1976, the worst in living memory and it bubbles forth still, into the shingle of the Bay, from its neglected old basin. In the adjacent track, dark, blood-red scraps of haematite may still be found, but the counting house and the former 'mine floor' (the ore dump from which the ships were loaded) has vanished under a veritable sea of nettles. The spring is badly neglected. Formerly, it flowed from a neat limestone basin, but now the pool is grubby, the stone surround misplaced or broken. It is a great pity, for the name of this spring, Beanwell, a corruption of the 'bene' (good well) was known to coastal sailors far and wide. Moreover, the source of the ore brought down to the Baycliffe mine floor was one of the richest haematite mines in the district. Baycliffe, despite its size, was very busy indeed in the 18th century.

A century before this, the gentle Quakers, followers of the redoubtable Margaret Fell and George Fox, were constantly robbed, sadly but quite legally within the laws of the time. Usually, this was at the instigation of the local clergy, who were enraged at the Quaker refusal to pay church tithes or attend the local parish church, despite being fined large sums of money, or having precious personal possessions or prized poultry, a valuable bull, pigs, or cattle all 'distrained'. Distraining was really a euphemism for a wicked and pernicious form of legal theft, for the goods obtained in this way were often of greater value than any fine demanded in cash. Some members of the established church had special people looking out for such goods, and then trumping up charges to appropriate them, paying these servants in cash or kind a percentage of the proceeds.

At Baycliffe, the church villains were centred on Aldingham, barely a mile away to the west. Despite all council of restraint by the elders, some of the exasperated Quakers finally showed their anger at such injustices, though by voice, and never by blow, to their persecutors. The account book of Sarah Fell, of Swarthmoor Hall, home of George Fox and his wife Margaret, provides a few fascinating items of the Baycliffe people letting off steam in Aldingham church against the oppressive incumbents!

Aldingham parish included several other hamlets and villages, so it was to this church that indignant Quaker wives and mothers from a wide area went to vent their anger on the cowering rector. One of these reverends was an avowed enemy of all Dissenters - people who did not agree with the established church. The priest was Thomas Shaw, who was rector of Aldingham from 1625 to 1667. He 'had some controversy' with the great Margaret Fell, while on the 24th March, 1654, 'Anne Clayton, late of Swarthmore, spinster'. was indicted at Lancaster for interrupting the parson at Aldingham with a cry of 'Come down thou greedy dog, woe unto thee!'. Another woman, who took the rector to task at the same time was 'Jane, wife of Richard Ashburner, of Gleaston'. who said, 'I am comen to bid thee come downe, thou painted beast ...'! While yet another, a visitor from Overkellet, across the Bay, tackled the quivering Shaw with 'Come down thou well-favoured harlot, thou deceivest this people ...!'. One male Quaker, Thomas Curwen, however, had the last word, for he recorded that 'Shaw ended his days in great Wo and Misery ... for the Lord laid his judgements upon him who was struck into a palsie ...'. It was written down almost with grim satisfaction, for the Lord has obviously punished their transgressor!

Shaw's successor at Aldingham was Theophilus Amyas, another parson determined to strike at the Quakers. Again, the Quakers bested him, for though he was '... another with his horns who began to push, and make war with the Lamb ...,' the sturdy local Dissenters were pleased to record that '... he was both blind and mad before he dyed ...!' He was followed by yet another of the same ilk called Michael Stanford, recorded by one local Quaker with contempt as 'driving on Pharaoh's chariot as fast as he can ...'!

Who would be aware of this religious turmoil when visiting either peaceful, stolid Baycliffe, or Aldingham church today? The old parish church is the very essence of tranquillity, with little disturbing the silence but the sea-wind and the sound of birds, which may include anything from the cawing of rooks in early spring in the elms of the old rectory, to the wild, sweet, sad flute of curlew, out on the Bay's mud flats at low tide. Aldingham church is dedicated to St. Cuthbert, a Saxon saint, and there is a tradition that here, his coffined corpse rested briefly during that long 8th century travail of monks carrying it, seeking safe rest for Cuthbert's saintly body; frightened but faithful men trying to find a place free from Viking attack. The Norsemen drove them from Lindisfarne, and, according to folk tale, they wandered the country for years before finally coming to rest at Durham.

Cuthbert was a Saxon saint, and the name Aldingham is definitely of that race. It means the place of the Alds, but there is no village here, even though one Ernulf owned and ploughed 'six carucates of land' according to the Domesday Book of 1086. This was a considerable holding, for a carucate is an area of land 'able to be ploughed by a team of oxen in a year'. Other than the ancient church, there is little at Aldingham now but a marvellous mansion built in 1845 by a very rich vicar. He left it, and much of his estate, to his butler who promptly opened up a shipbuilding yard in Ulverston and made another fortune! The vicar also built the stout sea wall, a feat remembered by the date stone set in the limestone. This barrier is the sole protection of church and churchyard against direct attack by the sea. The church itself is Norman, and is built in two parts, the eastern end being much older. There, behind the altar, is a hole in the wall (now glazed), which, by tradition, was where bread and wine was handed out to poor lepers, who dared not enter or approach the church in any other way. Inside, there is a hagioscope, or peephole between the western half and the narrow eastern part. It enabled the congregation on that side of the church to see what was going on at the altar and is a feature of many old churches.

There are many interesting features in this lovely, cool old building. The pillars, for example, are marked out in massive blocks carved and cut to fit neatly together. In reality, each huge pillar is one complete piece of stone, weighing several tons and demanding great engineering skill to place in position. How were these huge pillars carved and erected with such precision?

Close by the church front door is an ancient and badly weathered carving; the gravestone of Goditha de Scales, a prioress of some unknown religious house and the sister of the first Norman overlord to arrive here. Less than a mile away and half destroyed by the sea are the remains of the motte and bailey (a rudimentary but effective fortress of turf and timber) built by Michael le Fleming, plus evidence of his later dwelling surrounded by a ditch, at the obviously named Moat Farm, close by the winding coast road.

Michael came here late; in 1107, in fact, not 1066. Nor was he a powerful baron. In fact, it is very likely that he was a poor relation of more powerful Normans who came to England with the Conqueror 41 years earlier. This was typical of Henry I, the astute and avaricious son of William, who was well aware of the constant threat to his north-western lands. They were attacked from the sea by Irish and other pirates, and from the north overland by the tribes beyond the Border. By granting land to the poorer Norman and Flemish squires, he could ensure their loyalty, and at the same time, keep away those who threatened his rule in the north. Michael, in modern terms, was a Belgian, as the term le Fleming indicates and probably a sheep farmer used to wilder and rougher land than his wealthier relations. He policed an avowed Saxon area on a rather dangerous and hostile frontier. Proud Normans ate wheaten bread, refusing inferior fare; their poor cousins were more used to barley and oats, which was probably an additional reason why those of inferior rank were 'imported' to oversee the poorer northern English and Lowland Scots land.

The grassy mound on which Michael le Fleming built his sturdy timber *donjon*, or tower, remains, but approximately half is now missing, washed away by the tides. Barely recognisable are relics of the moat and turf walls once surmounted by pointed staves to guard the bailey. The quarters for the men and their attendants, are also present, grassed over and hard to see.

The later le Fleming house was a square tower, built two hundred yards inshore from the present coastline, but only the weedy ditch which was once the moat surrounding it can now be seen; it gave a name to the present Moat Farm alongside.

The lowly le Fleming family, founders of the later and the more powerful line of the Lords of Aldingham, gave way to successors living inland, at Gleaston Castle, another ruin still to be seen. Michael, however, had much of his power taken away, by order of the king, as soon as Furness Abbey established a hold on the district. He kept his lands, but he was told quite plainly that the Abbot was to be considered as his overlord. Michael protested, but bowed, eventually, to the inevitable. Fleming is still a common surname in Furness, and one of the later more powerful antecedents made his home at Coniston Hall, the same family going on to live at Rydal and taking a prominent part in 17th century affairs, both local and national.

Beyond Moat Farm, travelling west, the road begins to close with the sea. Several times in later years, it has been badly damaged by winter storm, particularly near the quaintly-named Goadsbarrow. The Goad family were prominent Quakers in Baycliffe, but the surname, still present in that village and elsewhere locally, is very old. It means a cattle drover. One member of this family, a veteran of the Civil War, crossed the sands regularly with a stock of cattle in his care, bound for the markets of Lancaster, in the latter half of the 17th century. Newbiggin, another hamlet not far away, was perhaps once a small grange of Furness Abbey. Seed Hall, the name of an old house there, is perhaps a relic of the monk's agricultural activity, but there is little of historical interest. The road here is barely above the shore and makes a magnificent drive. It carries on, heading due west and climbing briefly before descending again almost to sea-level and Rampside.

This is a sprawling linear village, with most buildings on the northern half of the road, and in much of the village nothing but the sea wall edging the road to keep away the violence of heavy seas. Much of the shore is now silting up, the buildings facing a maritime prairie of tough spartina, a tall and pestilential sea-grass; a recent invader which is rapidly replacing sand and salting formerly loud at all seasons with bird call.

Rampside is a lovely name. It means 'Hrofni's saetr', the farm where the cattle were taken in late spring and summer to enjoy the new grass, and owned by a Norseman called Hrofni (Raven). Was this Rampside Viking dark, hawk-nosed, and fierce, like his avian namesake, the bird of Odin? We shall never know, but a Viking sword, possibly even his, was found in the soil of Rampside churchyard, a mile away. Mind you, as proof of the age of

The seafront bungalow at Rampside where Wordsworth once spent a holiday. Now divided into two dwellings

Rampside is the 'Seaman's Church', with many mariners buried here

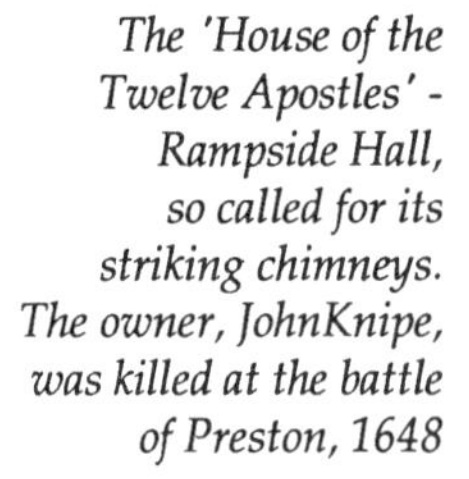

The 'House of the Twelve Apostles' - Rampside Hall, so called for its striking chimneys. The owner, JohnKnipe, was killed at the battle of Preston, 1648

such human settlement, so was a Bronze Age burial, a Neolithic stone axe from the Langdale factory site, and a medieval gravestone set in the church wall and still on view! Rampside is the 'seamen's church', for many a mariner is buried here. Some died of "Yellow Jack" a terrible fever; others of malaria, or blackwater fever, caught in other places and other climes. One was a giant Negro, brought ashore in a huge casket, and so, the story says, buried doubled up in his crude planked coffin!

The oldest house in Rampside is the Hall, mainly Jacobean in date, with a flamboyant but undated 'Yorkshire doorway'. This part is the rebuilding or replacing of an older structure still; dating back before the days of Good Queen Bess. Known variously as the 'House of the Twelve Apostles', or the 'House of Twelve Chimneys', the house does, in fact, have a dozen smoke stacks sitting on the roof ridge like so many square, squat pigeons! Rampside Hall, mainly 17th century, formerly the seat of another branch of the Knipe family. The Knipes were not Dissenters, nor Roundheads, but stoutly Catholic and Royalist. One member of the family, John Knipe, was killed at the Battle of Preston, in 1648, fighting for the King. In those days, there was a huge wood, well stocked with deer and game of all kinds at the back of the house, covering an area which is now no more than bald, grassy fields. Today, tall trees of any kind are comparatively scare and highly localised in much of Low Furness. They are especially so here, by the tide; which is what one would expect in such a windblown area.

There are three islands offshore. Two are tidal, the third now joined to the mainland by a long causeway. First there is Foulney, a Norse word meaning Island of wildfowl - a rapidly eroding island with little attached human history although there was a house here in the 17th century, and I can well remember the island as summer grazing for post-war Rampside cattle. The foundations of a medieval 'oyster-pen' on the western shore finally vanished several years ago.

There may have been some very early inhabitants of Foulney. Several Roman coins have been found, dating from the second and third centuries and these cause interesting speculation. Did the Romans ever have a marine station on Foulney? An outpost manned by marines, or members of the 'Classis Britannica', the Roman Navy of Great Britain? On nearby Walney a slab of slate, on which is scratched the markings for the game of nine men's morris (one variety of which was very popular in Roman times) was found on the south end of the island, indicating perhaps a Roman signalling station. Do the Foulney coins betray the presence of another Roman unit? Perhaps they were the Picti - the Painted Ones (not to be confused with the "Pictae", the Picts from beyond the Scottish Border). The "Picti" were sailors clad in sea-green uniform, who manned very light, fast craft painted similarly and used to approach and identify any strange craft in Roman waters. Quite possibly, such a group were stationed at Lancaster, with small units posted about the mouth of the Bay to watch for possible intruders. Nowadays, with so much concentration on so many parts of the natural environment, such interesting historical possibilities (or fancies?) tend to be forgotten, and it must be admitted that the evidence for Roman presence on the northern edge of the Bay is decidedly slight.

In spring and summer Foulney, the 'Island of Wildfowl', certainly earns the title, for on this stretch of shingle and grass, scarce 10 feet above high tide, thousands of birds will nest. Most are those magical 'sea swallows', the terns; summer immigrants, some arriving here from more than half a world away. The two major species are the common and Arctic terns, immigrants from feeding grounds in the South Atlantic and the edge of Antarctica respectively. Sandwich terns may also nest on Foulney, but these, here from West Africa and the largest tern species breeding in Britain, are erratic nesters. Some years they settle briefly on Foulney, others, they do not. The rarest species, the roseate tern, breast flushed with pink in breeding dress, is also an erratic breeder here, but at best, it seems an increasingly rare species throughout its northern summer range. The last of the five tern species is the hardy little tern, about the size of a starling, nesting on the shingle of the foreshore, always in the eye of the wind; breeding here precariously after wintering in North Africa. This important tern breeding ground is now carefully wardened each summer.

In the shorter days, Foulney makes an excellent platform for watching the many species of waders frequenting this end of Morecambe Bay; apart from whole clouds of dunlin and knot, there are a host of other species present then. Golden and grey plover, sanderling, curlew by the thousand, whimbrel, hordes of oystercatchers and piping redshank, godwits, and many more regard Morecambe Bay as their winter retreat. From Foulney, when the time and tide are right, one may see the passing pageant of these birds, with the certain knowledge of lots of wildfowl as bonus, plus a strong chance of seeing rarities.

Roa Island (*Roa* here means red) is a cluster of houses, a lifeboat station, and a boat pier converted to a sailing club. The houses are Victorian, but a castellated cobble building on the west shore, now a chapel, was once the Rampside Customs House, built in 1845.

Due south of Roa, barely half a mile away, is Piel Island, complete with lovely old pub alongside a mouldering old sandstone castle ruin. Once, this was 'Fodderey', the 'Fodder Island', but now it is Piel, the name owing a lot

The old Customs House at Roa Island was built in 1845.
It is now used as a chapel

Piel Castle where Lambert Simnel landed in 1487 to try and capture the throne of England

to the pele, the 14th century fortress built on the island. It was built in the 1300s, and though 1327 has been stated as the year of building, this is doubtful. More than one historian has suggested a date after 1348, the year of the Black Death. Some say that imported Irish labour was used, because the Furness population had been so devastated by the terrible bubonic plague that they could not look after themselves, much less build a castle.

Originally, Piel was in charge of the Abbot of Furness, as a fortress protecting Furness from the sea, and it does indeed bestride the entrance to Walney channel and Barrow harbour, guarding the southern approaches. It may well have replaced an earlier turf and timber fortress, and though the stone replacement was intended as a manned castle, it was never one holding armed men for very long. It was used by the Abbot as a warehouse for wool exported to Flanders, though smuggled is a better word, for a succession of abbots, working closely with equally wily Flemish wool merchants on the Continent, never paid dues to the reigning king. More than once the abbots were threatened with prompt royal punishment. They were particularly successful during the reign of Henry VI, when the country was being torn apart in the early years of the Wars of the Roses. A succession of abbots managed to evade either customs tariff or punishment, the Abbey enjoying a brisk shipping trade in all manner of goods from and to Piel for many years. At one time, the Abbey owned at least one ship; she was the *Mari Cogge,* a cog or cogge being a deep-bellied trading vessel.

The most exciting time in the history of the castle was in June, 1487. In that month, the supposed son of the late Duke of Clarence (Yes! That one drowned according to Shakespeare 'in a butt of Malmsey wine'!) landed here from Ireland to claim for the crown from Henry Tudor, whose army had recently defeated and slain Richard III, last of the Plantagenets on Bosworth Field. This new claimant to the crown was an impostor; Lambert Simnel, son of an Oxford pastrycook, put forward by the Yorkist faction in a final and desperate attempt to seize the throne from the Lancastrians. Simnel landed on Piel and the mainland with about 8,000 troops, 3,000 of them German mercenaries commanded by the Captain Schwarz mentioned earlier in connection with the place-name 'Swarthmoor'. The rest appeared to be Irishmen, loyal but untrained and badly armed rabble. The Abbot of Furness Abbey, wisely as it turned out, refused to be implicated.

Simnel, at the head of his mainly ragged and irregular army, marched on to Stoke Field in the Midlands, to be soundly defeated by the forces of Henry Tudor after a terrific struggle. Sir Thomas Broughton, the sole aristocrat from Furness to throw in his lot with the Yorkists, escaped from the battlefield. Deprived in his absence of all his estates, considered dead by most, he led an outlaw's life fed and looked after by loyal tenants for several years in the dense woods of his own estate of Witherslack, across the Leven Sands, just over the old Lancashire border into Westmorland. Eventually, dying in his own deep forest, he was buried there, at a site now lost to human memory.

Lord Lovell, companion leader to Sir Thomas, had a more terrible fate. He disappeared during the battle, and was never seen again. Just over two centuries later, in 1708, during demolition work at Minster Lovell Hall in Oxfordshire, workmen found '... the entire skeleton of a man, as having been at a table which was before him with a book, paper, pen ... all much moulder and decay ...'. This was a secret chamber which the workmen had broken into, and it was supposed that Francis, Lord Lovell, had hidden himself there after escaping Stoke Field; afterwards dying of starvation, never daring to call for help, ever fearful of discovery. It was a terrible end for a man once one of a powerful trio consisting of himself, Catesby and Ratcliffe; most trusted of Richard III's ministers.

Piel Castle, with its association of monastic-smugglers, outlawed aristocrats, and Yorkist pretender to the throne, is a fascinating place. Freely open to the public, it is accessible by summer ferry from Roa Island.

Piel, described delightfully in the 16th century as '... a lytell ylond herd upon the see syde and in the mowth of a ffair avon, that drawith VI ffadom depe at low water ...', guards the approach to the harbour and town of Barrow-in-Furness. This is neat and bustling; a place of wide streets, and about the town centre, shows a typical grid-iron pattern of Victorian terraced houses. The town hall is immense, a huge sandstone pile of Victorian Gothic topped by a 190-foot tower; overall, it resembles the large town hall of Manchester. Barrow, like Middlesbrough and Fleetwood, was a deliberate Victorian creation; a bold new town, right on the tip of the Furness peninsula, growing from a village of something like 40 inhabitants in the 1840's to a fully fledged borough in its own right by 1887. Today it has a population of about 55,000.

Barrow is approached by a four-mile, tree-lined road as wide and as well designed as a modern motorway, but built a hundred years before its time. It is the most Lancastrian of all that part of the county which was swallowed up by Cumbria in 1974. There is no dialect to speak of, but it has a speech reflecting more the flatter tones of Lancashire rather than any hint of Westmerian or true Cumbrian and a native sense of humour which is matched only by Liverpool. Barrow is a shipbuilding town; one which builds warships and now concentrates on submarines. Much of the town, and its economy, is associated with VSEL, the Vickers Shipbuilding and

The ruins of Furness Abbey. When the Abbey was closed in 1537 chaos descended on southern Lakeland, where it had ruled for 400 years

Engineering Company Limited, with a present payroll of something like 12,000 men and women plus a veritable army of people employed by various sub-contractors. Despite such heavy industry, Barrow is neither smoke-ridden nor a concrete jungle. Indeed, few towns of its size and type of industry can boast of such marvellous surroundings; rolling green hinterland, miles of sandy seashore, and tall sand dunes minutes away from the town centre. The Lakeland mountains are less than 20 miles away by road, and within three miles from the town hall is one of the loveliest abbey ruins in the whole country; but then, I am biased!

The ruins are those of Furness Abbey; once the most powerful religious house in all Britain except for Fountains Abbey, its closest rival, over in Yorkshire. Founded in 1127 as a Benedictine monastery, Furness was changed to the more powerful Cistercian order within a few years. By the time of its dissolution in 1537, it held lands which stretched far and wide throughout Furness and Lakeland; thousands of acres which included areas up to the very foot of the central Scafell massif, and beyond, into Borrowdale, with connections or property from the Isle of Man to southern Ireland. Its influence on the Furness economy lasted for more than 400 years, and when it went, for a while at least, the countryside was in chaos.

The ruins are truly beautiful; warm red sandstone buildings on emerald green lawns and turf as soft as velvet. No description could give it justice, a visit is necessary. Look for the multitude of mason's marks, the crudely scratched pattern of a nine men morris board on the steps of what was a guest-house, and the carving of salmon and other fish on the internal wall of the same place. Furness Abbey is unique, and has a history which would take days in the telling. There is but one way to satisfy any curiosity of it; go there, and look!

5: The Long Island

WALNEY ISLAND, a long, low hump of grass, boulder clay, sand dunes and sea-borne stones, is shaped like some gigantic, stranded whale. It guards the south-western flank of the Furness peninsula against the perpetual rollers of the Irish Sea; it is a slim land barrier, fatter in the middle, ever under threat from the tides; a battleground in the constant struggle between marine erosion and deposition.

The suffix "ey" in "Walney" betrays a Viking origin of this ancient place-name. "Ey" is common in the old Norse tongue; it means "island", but what of the rest, the prefix? Was Wal-ney originally the old Norse "Vogn-ey", the "Island of the Killer Whale", from some fancied resemblance to that giant, pied dolphin with a mouthful of wicked teeth? Or is the island named after 'Hougun', a pre-Conquest thrall of Tostig, treacherous brother to the Saxon king, Harold Godwinsson? Tostig, Earl of Northumbria, (killed by his more famous brother at the battle of Stamford Bridge, prior to the vital battle of Hastings) was undisputed owner of this wide northern land before King William of Normandy claimed it for his own. Yet another suggestion for the origin and meaning of the island's name is "Walna-ey", the "Walled Island", which does not appear to bear closer examination. No one, it seems, knows the true origin and meaning of the place-name, but personally, I favour "Hougun-ey", the island of that long dead and virtually unknown Saxon thrall of the wicked Earl of Northumbria.

Walney, including its hooked southern tip, is about 11 miles long, give or take a few hundred yards either way according to the current state of erosion or deposition. It is a relic of the Ice Ages, which shaped and formed the present topography of Furness. It is split from the mainland by Walney Channel, a stretch of shallow water filled and emptied twice every day by the ebb and flow of the tides. The island soil, now largely boulder clay but probably once including fertile 'brown earth' created by former tree cover, plus peat and blown sand, was an ideal and productive mixture. Indeed, almost within living memory, Walney was the 'Granary of Furness'.

The island was then being cultivated by villagers of two ancient and rival island settlements, both huddled on a lee shore, on the eastern side of the island. Close by the Channel and thus away from the constant onshore wind and threat of the Irish Sea, Biggar is the village to the south, while North Scale is on the north-eastern edge. Today, much of the central part of

Walney - the sea is ever present and there is a constant growl of surf on the western shore

Walney has disappeared beneath neat houses and new estates, the remaining farmland now reduced mainly to grazing. Yet, despite any development, much of Walney retains both charm and challenge. The sea is ever-present, the growl of surf on the western shore of this long island a lullaby to past and present generations of young Barrovians on every stormy night.

For those who love wild and windblown places, however small, this western beach can be a constant source of wonder and fascination. The twice-daily tides, scattering man-made rubbish typical of any shore today, may also deposit many strange or bizarre objects on the strand, such as *Loligo,* the goggle-eyed Atlantic squid, a powerful, ten-armed hunter. Perhaps a bulky grey seal may be seen, or the slimmer dog-like common species. In hot summers, the water may be full of sea-gooseberries, iridescent globules of living jelly, harmless and lovely, or, on rare occasion, hold the body and four-metre long stinging tentacles of Portuguese man o'war, a stunningly beautiful jellyfish, coming from warmer seas.

In September, it is possible to swim in a darkened sea illumined by a myriad pin pricks of electric blue and vivid green light, the warning signals of a tiny planktonic organism called *Gonylaux*, which lights, momentarily, every water movement. But this phenomenon shows only on moonless nights, with a tide as black and as smooth as oil. In broad daylight, the tide's edge bears a faint red tinge from this unique plankton. Elsewhere in the world, often in warmer seas, it masses into so-called 'red tides', sudden 'blooms' of toxic plankton which may kill fish and poison filter-feeders such as shellfish in massive numbers. Indeed, it has been suggested that such a red tide was the first of the ten Plagues of Egypt, wherein, according to the Bible, Exodus Chapter 7, verses 20 and 21:

> "... all the water that was in the river was turned into blood, and the fish that was in the river died, and the river stank ... and the Egyptians could not drink of the water of the river; and there was blood throughout all the land of Egypt ...".

In North America, there is a tradition that long before the arrival of the white man, the Indians stationed their own warriors on any beach flooded by the 'red tides', warning off those who attempted to gather shellfish rendered quickly toxic by this strange and yet beautiful mass of plankton. However, the faint-hearted should be re-assured that there is no chance of any such event occurring on the long island!

A month after the strange bioluminescence (living light) of *Gonylaux*, late October gales hurl masses of debris, natural and man-made, onto Walney's westerly shore. Together with a blanket of *Flustra* (fawn-coloured seaweed-like flattened strips, covered in a tiny honeycomb pattern), the storm brings in masses of thongweed, casting it on the beaches like some gigantic, raggy, brown rope, hundreds of yards long. Amongst this one may find the ugly

Aphrodite - the Sea Mouse - is actually an irridescent marine worm, often revealed by October gales on the Walney foreshore

'Sea mouse', christened by a witty and cynical taxonomist 'Aphrodite', after the ancient Greek goddess of love. It is not a mouse, but a marine worm, and though ugly of body and shape, it gleams with a rainbowed iridescence which is truly breathtaking.

The beach, and the offshore water, is full of surprises. According to the luck and patience of the observer and, of course, the season. There may be gannets plunge-fishing in the tide races; or, towards the end of the nesting season on cliffs further to the north, rafts of dark guillemots and razorbills floating close inshore. Much more rarely, and only with considerable luck, one might see the tall sail-fin of a basking shark, as much as forty feet long in the male, but in reality a harmless titan, a gentle, sluggish giant armed with tiny teeth, sieving plankton from the sea while cruising, mouth agape, at a humble maximum speed of two knots! I photographed, years ago, a dead baby of this species, trapped in the water of an ebbing tide and finally abandoned by a frantic mother as the water shallowed too rapidly to allow any help. Though the young basking shark was probably not much more than four months old at most, it measured 6 feet 10 inches nose to tail, and had an estimated weight of more than a quarter of a ton! Another strange discovery, this time in the mud of the beach, was a 'cockle-rake'; a red deer antler, discarded by a Mesolithic hunter-gatherer thousands of years ago as he sought to dig the cockles from the sand. He, and his folk left other traces in the earth and dunes of the long island.

At low tide, on the seaward side, there are ever-changing tidal pools, with crabs, which range from the very common green shore species to the tiny hermits, each in its own chosen shell. Also present at one and the same time may be the huge, bright pink oval-carapaced edible crab, or 'Billy Bones', as the local longshoremen call it. This is a sturdy swimming crab, with long legs broadened and modified into paddles! There are dog-whelks, slow but remorseless hunters of barnacle or mussel, with shells coloured according to which of these they eat; white for the barnacle-eaters, grey brown for the winkle-hunters, and blue brown for devourers of clinging mussels! There are chitons, aptly named 'Coat-of-mail shells', which are not shellfish, but a different family altogether, seemingly, at low tide, glued to cobble or boulder, and looking like legless, heavily-armoured wood-lice.

There are also seaweeds of olive-brown, glistening black, emerald or bottle or lime green, crimson and scarlet; millimetres, centimetres, or metres long according to species. They come in all shapes and sizes; thongs of dark brown, broad straps over six feet long, delicate and filmy sheets of soft plastic, dark green and furry tufts. Some are blood-red, bleaching to small, chalky coralline sprays in bright sunlight. Indeed, for those who care to look, this shoreline is a fascinating, tiny cosmos in itself. Every day brings change, each of the twice-daily tides presenting new charm and puzzle.

The face of the sea itself is also subject to constant alteration of light, form and colour. One moment, perhaps, grey and sullen, apparently empty of life. Or clay-brown, foam flecked with cream; the surface changed to brilliant, glittering blue or brightest jade by roving beams of sunlight. In sudden gale it is rapidly altered to a heaving, dour monotone, flecked and spattered with white in a turmoil of wild water. Then, it becomes magnificent; a shrieking wind sends forth flurries of stinging spindrift and spume to splatter over shining beach cobbles. Huge breakers crash onto the land; the shore takes a mighty battering, the edge of the tide becoming a temporary maelstrom where giant combers thunder continuously onto the beach. Spent waves snatch back gravel and shingle in the snarl and growl of fierce undertow, each great mass of water retreating rapidly to reform yet more giant waves.

When such storm is over, and the sea a muted, oily ground-swell, the waders come in. Lines of huddled oystercatchers, bleating shrilly to the wind; hysterical redshank screeching ever of danger, turnstones picking amongst the sea-tangle, dumpy knot and smaller dunlin, ringed plover moving about like so many clockwork toys are all there. Sometimes, particularly in spring or autumn, there are other kinds, like grey plover or purple sandpipers, godwits, whimbrel, or near-white sanderling dancing

One of Walney's many migrants - a ruff

at the breakers' edge. Walney, particularly the western shore, plays host to thousands of birds; including a marvellous record of rare and unusual species. Recently, in early autumn, at one shallow freshwater pool in the south of the island several uncommon species were recorded together including ruff and reeve, curlew sandpipers, a little stint scarce the size of a sparrow, a pair of green sandpipers and a 'wisp' of seven snipe pausing here on their passage south from high northern latitudes. Another year, amongst several other species, I saw greenshank, and a gale-blown hooded crow.

Beyond the tiny hamlet of Biggar, the South Walney Nature Reserve becomes the noisy breeding ground every spring and summer of thousands of gulls. It is the largest gullery of its kind in Europe, in which the herring gull and the lesser black backed gull breed cheek by jowl (or should it be 'cheek by beak'?) with nests (each little more than an untidy scrape in the ground) crowding the turf and sand of fossilized sand dunes. Each and every spring, the whole area becomes a raucous, bustling avian slum, filled rapidly with squalling birds of incredible beauty. Such are the nesting pressures that some birds, either late arrivals, or more likely, first nesters, are forced on to the shingle of the shore above high water mark. In the centre of these old dunes, great black backed gulls breed every year, and amongst them are the eiders. These Roman-nosed ducks breed by the hundred on and around the Reserve, the hatched ducklings running the gauntlet of the opportunist gulls. These predators are on their way to the duck 'creches' on the surface of the inshore sea, where a few female eiders may look after dozens of very young birds. The quarrelsome gulls attack anything intruding into their immediate territory, which in the nesting pairs, is a circle of roughly six feet in diameter about the untidy nest. The adults will attack and often kill and eat anything small and defenceless venturing into the nesting area - including careless young pullets of the neighbours, even if they be of the same species!

At the Bird Observatory, within the Reserve, many thousands of birds are recorded each year. A large number are trapped, ringed, recorded and set free, for Walney lies right across the coastal migration route for many species of birds; those coming north in the spring, and those pouring out of the north and going south in late summer and autumn, plus many others blown off course in storm, or carried inland by contrary winds. By observing, trapping and recording, the Observatory has built up a huge record of rare and unusual species. To mention but a few these include stork, osprey, spoonbill and melodious warbler; the latter miles off course, but still closer to its normal breeding grounds in southern Europe than the straying paddyfield warbler, ringed on Walney in September 1982, presumably blown off course on the way to wintering grounds in northern India, Iran or southern Afghanistan!

The Reserve, besides its teeming birdlife, has other treasures. Flowers such as viper's bugloss, each plant a tall spire of vivid cornflower blue; and henbane, with beautiful creamy blooms etched and patterned in chocolate-brown; delicate and lovely flowers spoilt by stickiness, unpleasant smell, and the suggestion that this was the plant used by Dr Crippen to poison his wife! There are dune pansies, in purple, yellow and white; hound's tongue, cousin to the forget-me-not, but with deep red, glorious flowers carrying a musty smell of mice. It appears with bloody crane's bill, *Geranium singuinem*, masses of the clover-coloured blooms covering the drier shingle and scanty turf.

There are yet more bird species on the 'Spit', a curving bar of shingle, driven and dumped by tide-flow to form a long hook on the southern tip of the island leading in towards Morecambe Bay. Here, every spring and summer, there is a huge colony of terns, aptly called 'Sea-swallows' because of their aerial grace and superb flight, but also known as 'Birds of Light'. This wonderful name is quite correct when applied either to the Arctic or common species. Both will winter far beyond the Cape of Good Hope on the tip of South Africa, the common terns way down in the South Atlantic, the Arctics (which may nest as far north as the Arctic Circle, or even beyond it, hence their name) will fish during much of our northern winter at the very edge of the Antarctic ice-cap.

As with all migrants, their lives are governed by the seasons, and it is this which gives them their other and more romantic title, the 'Birds of Light'. They nest in our summer in the north, and flying south beyond the equator, spend our winter in the southern summer. When days begin to shorten with the onset of autumn in either hemisphere, the birds head in the other direction, following the longer days, enjoying the extended daylight! Terns travel many thousands of miles each year of their lives; the Arctic tern, following the whale-paths in the sea, where plankton and fish, welling up from the depths in cold, mineral-rich water appear in quantity, travels some 11,000 miles each way every year; plus a tremendous lot of flying to wherever oceanic or offshore feeding is best. These tough little birds may also live much longer than many other species. One common tern, ringed on Walney in 1935, was found dead in the same area in the south of the island in 1960! A bird quite definitely 25 years old! Imagine the sea-miles this tiny scrap must have travelled in all those years. The mind boggles!

South Walney has another interesting feature in the sturdy, white-

This 18th century lighthouse on South Walney is one of the oldest in Britain and still in use

painted lighthouse. This is one of the oldest lighthouses in Britain, it is the sole manned lighthouse on the Cumbrian coastline, and the furthest north on the western coast of England. Indeed, by now, it is the oldest manned lighthouse of all in this country! The keeper is a woman, one of a family who have looked after this powerful light for very many years. Walney Light was built in 1790, a 70-foot tower then costing £1,100 with a light of 3,500 candlepower. Nearby Barrow was then a creek port of Lancaster, as were Greenodd and Ulverston, so the lighthouse was built by the Lancaster Quay Commissioners to safeguard ships entering and leaving Morecambe Bay. The Royal Navy, coal vessels, and those bound for Lancaster, were freed of any harbour dues. Others, either sheltering stormbound in the area or 'neither loading nor discharging cargo' paid a penny a ton. Though the old port of Lancaster is now silted up and no longer accessible to larger vessels, nor is Barrow a busy harbour, Walney Light is still a very necessary part of the coastal system, even though it is not part of Trinity House. The 30 million candlepower light, almost a thousand times more powerful than the original, throws a white beam over the Irish Sea every 15 seconds from sunset to sunrise. It can be seen from many miles away on clear nights. Together with the braying foghorns used when visibility is limited, Walney Light, after more than two centuries of constant use, remains a vital part of the warning system to all west coast shipping.

Along the road north, away from the Reserve, the sandstone village of Biggar seems to crouch under the sea-wind. Like so many similar places, it is now a dormitory village, a popular place in which to settle. Many of the older houses have either gone or been altered out of all recognition, but the old pub still retains much of its character, as does the ancient barn opposite. This was a farming settlement once, and until the Dissolution of the monasteries in 1537, it was a thriving grange of Furness Abbey, an outlying farm where crops and cattle were raised. One of the staples grown was barley, which gave its name to the village long before the arrival of the monks, *bigg* is the old name for barley, while the *ar* at the end of the place-name is a corruption of *ergh*, a Norse-Irish title for a shieling, or a shepherd's bothy. Local legend, of uncertain date but going back a very long way, insists that once there were no houses here with windows facing the sea, in case a stray light betrayed the settlement to passing pirates!

There are also dark hints that the trade of wrecking was not unknown here. In this nefarious business ships were lured inshore by false harbour lights, to ground in the surf and be boarded, looted, and their bewildered crews killed by ruthless wreckers. Happily, there seems to be no truth in this grim legend as far as Walney is concerned. However, of several old skeletons discovered on the beaches over the years, most probably those of storm-drowned mariners, none bore any scrap of clothing, footwear, or jewellery!

More tangible evidence of human activity lies in the bank which borders the road north from the village, along the Channel edge. This is all that remains of Biggar Dyke, built originally by 13th century Furness Abbey monks, aided by their Biggar village tenants, as both a sea wall against the tides and road (on the flattened top of the Dyke) across the marshes to the village.

While the centre of the island is pleasant enough, much of it is covered by houses of various kinds. These again are rich in local history for many of the streets have surprisingly unusual or strange names like Mikasa, Naiad, Amphitrite, Latona, Strathmore and Strathnaver. These are not fancy titles, given at the whim of some builder; they are a proud catalogue of ships built in Barrow shipyard - a long list of vessels ranging from Japanese battleships to British cruisers.

If, however, the visitor wishes to see more ancient history, it may be better to explore the north end of the island by way of North Scale, the other Walney settlement, where 17th century houses appear alongside modern dwellings. The first house encountered at the entrance of the village is dated 1694. Possibly, it belonged originally to the Lancaster family, perhaps the replacement of one destroyed 50 years earlier. For in 1644, during the bitter Civil War, the village, mostly sympathising with the Roundheads, was attacked by a force of Royalists and burned to the ground '... except two houses. One was a stone house ... the other straw thatch'd ...'. The sturdy villagers gave as good as they got. The previous day they had confronted bold Sir John Preston, leader of the Royalists, with a sharp volley of musket shot, killing '... his horse, ... and an officer of his own which was next to his, which coming unexpectedly, made the horse to run, and no more was done at that time ...'. Which might explain why the deserted village was put to the torch!

North Scale is also famous for another historical event which took place eight years later, in 1652. It is best described in the words of the victim, the redoubtable George Fox:

> '... I went over in a boat to James Lancaster's; as soon as I came to land there rushed out about forty men with staves, clubs and fishing poles, and fell upon me, beating and punching me, and endeavoured to thrust me backwards into the sea ... they laid at me again, and knocked me down and stunned me ... I looked up and saw James Lancaster's wife throwing stones at my face ... her husband, James Lancaster was lying over me to keep the blows and stones off my face ... the people had persuaded James Lancaster's wife that I had bewitched her husband ... I got to my feet ... but they beat me down again into the boat ... which James Lancaster observing ... he came into the boat with me and set me over the water from them ...'.

Poor Fox had scarcely time to recover his breath before being set upon and given similar treatment when he landed on the other side of Walney Channel! He had some consolation, however, when James Lancaster's wife later became a respected convert to Quakerism!

North Scale had its own lime-kilns, and strangest of all, at least a trio of freshwater wells which rose and fell with the tide! These have vanished, but were well recorded. It would seem that the fresh water actually floated on top of tidal water seeping through the island soil and shingle and unless the well-water was violently disturbed at this time, it was possible to draw sweet fresh water from the top layer without it being polluted by sea-salt from the incoming tide!

After North Scale, one of the best places to start any exploration of the north of the island is Ernse Bay. Pronounced *Ernsee*, it means the haunt of sea-eagles, but the last of that magnificent species about here was caught in the early 19th century, on the summit of Black Combe. The regal bird was caught on top of the mountain by a shepherd in 1838 '... and this is believed to have been the last sea-eagle captured on any of our mountains ...'.

There is little chances of ever seeing sea-eagles here today, but there are always the waders and other sea birds, the occasional over-wintering peregrine (often a first-year bird from further afield), miles of tawny sand at low tide, tall dunes, and a breathtaking panorama of the Lakeland hills

North Scale, Walney, showing the low-water ford over the channel to Barrow

spiking the northern and north-eastern skyline.

Unlike the south of the island, where the sandhills change more each year towards sandy heath, the northern dunes still bear the great open spaces of "blow-outs", where gales have ripped away the vegetation, and the sand is once more on the move. This is now being checked, for at one time such a gap threatened to split the island in two, an event which would soon cause rapid and disastrous further erosion on many sections of coastline beyond.

This sandhill complex is very rich in fauna and flora. That unique flower, the Lancashire geranium, *Geranium Lancastriense,* first grew here. A probable sport of bloody cranesbill, each bloom is clear shell pink streaked with vivid, hair-thin lines of scarlet. It is a vanishing species, much less common than when I first encountered it. Three hundred years ago (long before my time, I hasten to add!) it was plentiful, for specimens of it were sent all over England by a Quaker botanist, Thomas Lawson, once the curate of Rampside church.

There are many orchid species here, from early purples to the broad-leaved twayblade and marsh helleborines. Evening primrose here is nothing like its English namesake for it is an American escapee, a tall spire of lemon-coloured, large disc-shaped flowers. It may become a prolific weed. There are many other species of flowers, some of them threatened species, together with a host of grasses, fungi and lichens.

Of the mammals, there are hares, occasional fox, rabbits, hedgehog, mice and vole. Best prize of all, the small natterjack - a cold-blooded amphibian, the delightful sandhill toad - is existing here, almost at the edge of its northern range, a delightful rarity guarded very carefully. Short-eared owls, birds of vole-ridden heathland and daytime hunters, are predators of the grassier areas.

There are traces of man from small artifacts left by roving groups of Mesolithic folk, (the nomadic 'hunter gatherers' or 'hunter pastoralists' as they are now more often called) to the more organised and settled habitations of the first farmers of the New Stone Age and occupational remains of Bronze and early Iron Age smiths. The Mesolithic folk were on Walney perhaps 8,000 years ago. In small family groups, they hunted, fished and gathered everything from edible fungi to berries, birds' eggs, and shellfish. They left little behind but small stone tools, some of them made from flint gathered on the beaches, the honey-coloured rock washed as cobbles and pebbles from a chalk reef somewhere below the waves of the Irish Sea. At one place, now lost beneath a town tip there were clay hearths; places where gathered food was cooked. By such a spot, I found amongst a scatter of shells, the barbed tail of a thornback ray, which gave a clue to the time of its demise. These fish move into the shallower inshore waters to breed during early spring. Was this the season these people camped by the sea, harvesting by net, spear, harpoon gathering or trapping the rich animal sources either close by or in the sea? To survive, these hunting groups took everything and anything from harpooned porpoise to mussel, from deer to wild ox. At this site, by these early family fireplaces, a plentiful supply of shattered cobbles, mostly granitic, was found. It has been suggested that these were "pot-boilers" used in cooking; the stones heated red-hot in open fires, and then plunged into water-filled skin bags containing fish or meat to be cooked. The water boiled, the meal cooked; but the red-hot stones were shattered by the sudden immersion. Pottery then was useless in cooking, it was crude and unable to bear fire-heat, nor could it hold water. Was the leather-bag form of cooking - as known to be practised by some very primitive peoples, used here on Walney - an alternative to roasting food in the fire embers? At present, this is no more than an interesting hypothesis, for there is no evidence which may prove - or disprove - it!

Much more recent in time, but still very old, the remains of an ancient bloomery lie here still, half-buried in the sand, marking a site where hard-won iron-ore was smelted close by the shore. Haematite, blood-red and very rich in iron (as much as 62% in some Furness ores) was melted down in crude, clay pot furnaces. The fuel was probably birch-charcoal, with hand-driven bellows forcing air into the glowing embers, ensuring constant high temperatures and a burn-off of most unwanted sulphides.

In much the same area, but earlier, flint and other stone tools were worked on a boulder 'anvil'. Found in the dunes, surrounded by scores of stone chips and flakes, it is now preserved in the Barrow museum.

Also on the north end of Walney, the Neolithic people took stone axe rough-outs and made handsome polished stone axes of them. The rough-outs were made in the central Lake District, many of them in Great Langdale, where an 'axe factory' flourished for many years. The stone is a volcanic 'tuff', a fine grained, beautiful green stone with a metallic ring when struck. The rough-outs were patiently and beautifully smoothed and polished into magnificent tools, using beach or river sand. They were traded over a wide area of northern England.

But what does one make of a fine polished stone axe found on Walney, made of a stone called porcellainite? This is a limey mud baked aeons ago by volcanic action and found only in Northern Ireland. Does not the Walney axe prove trade across the Irish Sea? Trade of some four thousand or more years ago, by frail craft, perhaps crossing by the treacherous Scottish narrows between Larne and modern Stranraer?

Dare one also deny the skill of an earlier Stone Age folk who made 'microliths', tiny, razor-sharp flint chips, found by the hundred in the eroding clay cliffs of Walney? They were fitted originally into slotted wood to make crude but very effective sickles to cut the stalks of early wheat, or oats, or other edible and ancient wild grasses.

Altogether, Walney Island offers many simple treasures to those willing to look; but there is often little that is obvious (unless it be the gullery in the nesting season!), even though there is always much to be seen, and heard by those willing to practise that old adage "Look, and see; listen, and hear".

This is also true of yet another dune complex, not on the island but across a few hundred yards of water from Walney's north-eastern tip. The water at the north end of Walney Channel is always present whatever the state of the tide. It is a deep, dark pool called Scarf Gap and is well-named. *Scarf* is an old name for cormorant, and these dark sea ravens fish here regularly. At low tide, when the sand banks are exposed, these birds stand with wings outstretched and drying, in ragged and untidy groups. The tide race at the island end is rich fishing ground for them and other species. Mergansers, the tooth-beaked 'saw-bills' hunt for flounders and in summer, diving terns of four species look for darting, silvery shoals of sand-eels. Wildfowl, from goldeneye to pintail, from scoter to humble mallard, may be seen, as well as startling occasionals such as phalarope or longtailed duck from far Arctic waters.

A cluster of wooden huts almost on the mainland shore marks Lowsy Point, a name which belies the beauty of this place and defies translation. Once it was a loading point for haematite, brought laboriously by horse and cart from the Dalton mines of the 18th century, and loaded, with much labour, into flat-bottomed hulks beached on the sands. Careful search of the beach even now yields lumps of rich red ore, carved and polished into strange and wonderful shapes by the action of storm and sea. Immediately beyond the scattered huts of Lowsy Point is the dune complex, Sandscale (the sandy *skali* of some ancient Norseman - his bothy, a temporary shelter by sand and sea, in an ancient rabbit warren) a huge area of low dune and marshy heath. In the foreground of Lowsy Point, close by the trickle of its solitary and indifferent spring of fresh water, is a patch of ground which bears each and every August and September, a mass of purple autumn gentians. In June or July, or perhaps even into August, whole carpets of flowers, including such delights as ladies fingers, wild thyme, dune pansy, and honey-scented ladies bedstraw spread a mixed pot-pourri of perfume over the tawny sandhills and the wetter hollows, or 'slacks'. It is a sweet and lasting fragrance which may be detected and enjoyed many yards away downwind.

Sandhills are delightful places at any season. Here, at Sandscale, now National Trust property, a wide marsh to the south prevents the spread of the dune complex; this wetter land is a place over which courting snipe soar in spring, tail feathers spread wide in every headlong dive; the vibrating plumage making the 'drumming', or 'bleating' associated with this remarkable bird. Puffed up, proud little stonechats rattle a challenge from scrubby hawthorns, the repeated sound much like that made when hard seashore pebbles are clashed harshly together. Wheatears, full of enquiry, dance attendance on almost every human visitor crossing the summer dunes. At the same time, one may listen to the surprisingly loud chorus of dozens of natterjack toads, assembled and mating in a pool not far away. It is an uncanny sound, louder and later in the season than the quieter croaking of common toad and frog. From a distance it resembles the noise of many two-stroke motorbikes, each revving hard in turn before being ridden rapidly away! Even the occasional corpse or carcass of rabbit or mouse can be fascinating; frequently, it is taken over by orange-banded sexton beetles, which bury the dead animal in the soft sand surprisingly quickly. They lay eggs in a carcass heated-up by putrefaction; a warmth which hatches the beetle grubs straight onto a mass of food!

A sprawl of bramble and wild rose bushes mark the meeting place of dune and marsh, providing cover for warblers and other small birds. The flowers are distinctive; white, fragile and sweetly scented, these are burnet roses, which some say formed the badge of the ill-fated House of York, during the long and bloody Wars of the Roses. Others, beyond the Border,

Ancient dunes at Sandscale

insist that it made the original white cockade of Bonnie Prince Charlie in another doomed enterprise, the Rebellion of '45. Whatever the historical connections, the burnet rose is a delight; so are the seed cases, the glossy hips. Instead of the usual briar scarlet, they are a deep and glowing purple.

The Sandscale dunes are equally attractive in winter. Hares lie up in the shelter of bramble scrub, partridge coveys seek out the gravel in the dune valleys, or bask in early sunlight. The prize attraction, the natterjacks, are missing, buried deep in the sand, hibernating until early spring; but, with luck, one may catch a glimpse of sneaking fox, or in the dusk, find the broad pad marks of a hunting badger. Above all, there is the silence and stillness of the whole area. Every footfall is masked by the soft sand, and apart from the wind, the distant murmur of the sea, and an occasional bird-cry, very little breaks the silence of this tiny oasis of tranquillity.

Beyond Sandscale, the shoreline curves round in a wide sweep, towards the Victorian village of Askam, once yet another iron-making small town, and now sometimes referred to as 'Coronation Street by the Sea'! The shoreline is now the southern edge of the wide Duddon estuary. The Long Island, Walney, lies behind us, to the south-west. Even if unseen, it cannot be forgotten, for the onshore wind carries with it the sound of surf, gentle or savage as the weather dictates. At night, particularly in the dark of winter, the noise is a lullaby to many Barrovians, young and old!

6: Drumlin Country:
Some Villages Of Low Furness

THE GREAT ICE SHEET which covered so much of the north a million and more years ago, reformed and re-shaped the land below its massive weight. Hundreds, sometimes thousands, of feet thick, moving infinitely slowly, it depressed and squeezed the land beneath, pulverising the surface rock, moving in mighty and awesome procession to the south, riding up and down over the bumpy earth at far less than any snail's pace, but always with irresistible force and power. The ground rock below this giant crusher, flour-fine and mixed with ice-melt, was plastered thickly over the surface topography eventually, as the ice sheet receded, leaving behind a layer of 'rock flour' (a smooth clay composed of microscopically fine particles) but studded thickly with rock of all kinds in the shape of rounded cobbles and boulders. When the last ice-melt finally came, this plastered and moulded landscape, completely bald of all vegetation, was revealed as a series of huge whalebacked hills; giant earth-waves frozen into immobility; or better still, as a smooth ground swell, formed infinitely slowly below a mighty ocean of solid ice.

To the modern geologist these rounded, elongated hills are drumlins, a word probably from the old Irish *druman*, meaning a ridge. In a swarm they form a lumpy series of long, smoothly-rounded hills, called by the geomorphologist "a basket-of-eggs topography". Much of Low Furness, between narrow, eroding coastal plain and the high moors, has drumlins everywhere. Between these massive, ellipsoid hills are wide, flat-bottomed ancient river channels, relics of the last meltwater run-off from retreating ice. Very often, the broad shallow rivers once contained within them have been replaced by a narrow beck, a corruption of the old Norse *bekkr*, meaning stream, which by its usually smaller size in a typically wide meltwater valley is called a misfit stream. Here, where surface water is comparatively uncommon, such places have given rise to human settlement, much of it ancient. Other human habitation grew up close by the larger *kettles;* large or small hollows, first ground out by moving ice, and left water-filled as pool or tarn, first by the melting or stranded, remnant ice, and later, by natural drainage.

Urswick Tarn is such a place; an ancient kettle, a large sheet of water, perhaps 40 feet deep at most, reed-fringed and rich in wildlife. A hundred years ago, it covered an area of '14 acres, 1 rood, and 12 perches', though the same careful investigator warned that it would not be so for ever. The infill, by stream-borne silt and decaying vegetation, though slow, is very sure. The rate was carefully calculated by the scientists in 1853 to be half an inch a year, so the tarn will probably be completely filled by the year 2846 - but only if the sedimentation rate remains constant.

'Urswick' is from the old English *Urse-wic* meaning bison lake village, where the first homesteads evolved about a tarn where European bison, aurochs, the tall wild cattle, wild pig, deer and other wild animals of the prehistoric landscape came to drink. In this limestone country, where surface water is always at a premium, the presence of the tarn explains both the continuity of the village and why Urswick grew up about it in the first place. If one be quite correct, this part is Great Urswick; the complete village being in two parts. Great Urswick lies near or about the tarn and Little Urswick half a mile south. Both are fascinating; beside the complex recorded history, there is much to see on the ground or in the field hereabouts.

Take Great Urswick for a start. There seems little that is 'Great' in this cluster of old houses around the northern end of the tarn and indeed the name has nothing to do with size. It goes back to the early years of Furness Abbey, sometime in the mid-12th century, when Michael le Fleming was probably still living in his motte and bailey, at Aldingham. He was given much local land, and briefly, was all-powerful in the area. The sudden and rapid rise of Furness Abbey changed that; Michael was told, by the king and in no uncertain terms, that he was to pay homage to the Abbot of Furness, who was the new all-powerful force in Furness. By agreement and probably not without a lot of protest, which went unrecorded, Michael was allowed to keep Great Urswick, part of his original grant and the Abbey added the other half of the village, the present Little Urswick, in exchange for westerly sections of Michael's land. Le Fleming was also given the village of Bardsea, but parted with Roose and the area south of it as far as Rampside and the coast. This gave the Abbey monks the harbour of Piel, still one of the safest waters in the kingdom, as part of the agreement. Great Urswick is a modern name; first of all, Urswick was 'Michael's Urswick', a name soon corrupted by dialect into 'Muckle Urswick'. Muckle, meaning large, was then changed into 'Much' and finally altered to the modern 'Great' once local dialect fell out of regular use.

With such association, it is not surprising that the two Urswicks are so rich in historical material. The whole area, has firm connection with human settlement which goes back into prehistory. Beyond the village, across the

The so-called Druid's Circle on Birkrigg Common, Urswick. The double circle dates from about 2100 BC

tarn and over the hump of Birkrigg Common to the east, there is the most strident and startling reminder of this. It is a small, double circle of crudely shaped limestone boulders. Dated to about 2100 B.C., virtually circular, this small stone ring is the best example of its kind in the whole of the British Isles. Excavated twice, it revealed little; a small clay pot containing incinerated human bone, paving of the inner circle, and traces, in the burnt-red soil, of past giant fires.

Two hundred yards north-west is the tiny quarry which yielded the circle's boulders; heaped cobbles there came from the beach, probably carried thence in skin or wickerwork baskets, to form a material-dump drawn on by a prehistoric people arriving on the scene long after the circle was built. This later race, different to the original circle-builders, were the folk responsible for the paving of the inner circle, the hammered cobbles so laboriously and carefully fitted now unseen beneath an over-growth of sheep-cropped turf. Due south, a quarter of a mile away, a huge and solitary stone, possibly an outlier of the circle, may well have been a lunar or solar marker to it. Certainly the tiny south-western stone, one of the ten visible in the inner circle, marks the winter setting of the moon. Local tale speaks chillingly of human sacrifice, and accordingly, the place is called by most the 'Druid's Circle', with many dark tales told of it. Little is known of this eerie ground; no true purpose or explanation for its use or construction has even been proved. Even in these enlightened days, to those who scoff at old beliefs and dark superstitions, it keeps its aura of mystery, its age-old puzzle of purpose, and all the secrets of those people of so long ago. It was a burial site, but was it also lunar or solar observatory, seasonal calendar, meeting place, temple of local gods? In truth, no one knows.

Beyond the stone circle, lower on the seaward slope, are the cottages and farms of tiny Sunbrick, the *Swine-brake* of the Middle Ages; the slope where pigs once grubbed for acorns on a slanting forest floor. Sunbrick, with 17th century datestones, but built on a much older site, is just above Seawood, the relic of a once great forest. It is still well endowed with trees, and by the entrance to it from Birkrigg Common there is a quiet walled enclosure. This is a Quaker burial ground, a peaceful, sheltered, sunny spot wherein lie many Quakers of the 17th and early 18th century. Each and every one is in an unmarked grave, according to the fashion of early Quakers, who thought it vain to mark any such resting place, or eulogise or vulgarise any grave occupant by inscription on wood or stone memorial. There is also a persistent but doubtful folk-tale of an elephant burial here! Supposedly, a huge circus elephant attached to a show visiting Walney in 1911, died on that island during the night and was smuggled up here during the dark of the following evening to be buried within the Quakers' enclosure!

To the north-east of Urswick village on a rounded hill marking the skyline, is another prehistoric construction. This is Skelmore Heads; a proven hill fort, where in the summer of 1959, the mother of a schoolboy being proudly shown round this site found two roughed-out stone axes, lying in a crevice between two boulders. Two more axes were found at the same place a little later, all being part of a once-compact bundle. No less than six socketed bronze axe heads were found nearby in 1902, and roughed-out axes, a saddle quern (for grinding corn into flour by hand), fragments of Bronze Age pottery, a stone knife, a burial tumulus, and human and animal bones have all been discovered on the site or in the immediate neighbourhood.

South and west of Great Urswick, half-hidden and overgrown by ash trees, are the Urswick "Stone Walls", now thought to be the site of a Romano-British settlement, which has revealed several possibly Roman artefacts. As further evidence, perhaps, of Roman influence, or contact, some of the broken walls trace out a rectangular building, the shape a sudden change from the rounded, often irregular structures of the ancient Britons which are also there. This Stone Walls complex also contains the outline of a huge circular and typically native hut, as if to confound any archaeologist. No Roman fort or *vicus*, a civil settlement often found near Roman forts, has even been found in Furness, but if one existed, Urswick might be a likely contender for the site.

Yet another stark reminder of the age of the present village of Great Urswick lies within 200 yards of the old parish church. Built into a neat limestone wall is a large irregular slab, in shape rather like a crude gate post,

The Priapus Stone atUrswick. A relic of pagan fertility worship the stone was decorated every May Day until the early 19th century

or stoup so common in older farm walls throughout the district. Over 7 feet long, 2 feet 6 inches wide, and at least a foot thick, this mysterious slab has an estimated weight of some one and a quarter tons. It bears six holes at one end, five of them in a cluster into which fingers and thumb can be fitted perfectly. It is the *Priapus Stone;* a crude phallic symbol used long ago in ancient fertility rites. Until the late 1920s, this Urswick stone stood upright in the field alongside, alone and neglected. It was not always so. A diarist, in 1810, wrote of it as '... a rough piece of unhewn Limestone, which the inhabitants of Urswick were accustomed to dress as a figure of Priapus in Midsummer Day, besmearing it with Sheep Salve, Tar, or Butter, and covering it with rags of various dyes, the Head ornamented with Flowers ...'.

The cult of Priapus goes back into and possibly beyond the age of Classical Greece. It came originally from the Dardanelles and was always represented by a statue or other symbol of a grotesquely ugly man, a god of fertility, the son of Aphrodite. This cult was later very popular in some towns of Roman Italy. A House of Priapus, a kind of Roman pub was recently excavated at Herculaneum. There were still nuts in a bowl on the counter for the customers standing at the bar, but carbonized by the intense volcanic heat when the city was overwhelmed by the mighty eruption of Vesuvius in 79 A.D. Which makes one wonder just how long the Urswick Priapus Stone has been there? Who erected it? What people worshipped it?

The church, just beyond the Priapus Stone, is also on an ancient site. The present building is Norman, but there was a church here before then; possibly some of the present fabric is Saxon. The tough, squat tower is a

The tower of Urswick church probably also served as a defensive pele until the 15th century, when windows were added. The low, narrow door was also defensive

reminder of rougher days; the low, narrow doorway, and the thick walls suggest former use as a pele, not dissimilar to Dalton Castle, as shelter for villagers against marauding Scots. They came here twice in the great incursions of 1316 and 1322, led by Robert the Bruce, 'laying waste everything as far as Furness, ... and burnt that district whither they had not come before ... taking away all the goods of the district, with men and women as prisoners. Especially were they delighted with the abundance of iron they found ...'.

The Furness reminder of such Scots invasion - "Nowt good ever comes round Black Combe" - has a different version over to the east of 'Lost Lancashire', though it dates from a similar time in history. There was said to a naughty or wilful child: "Hush ... or the Black Douglas will get ye!". Black Douglas was another Scots raider; but he came in from the east, and after burning and looting Cartmel and district, went south over the Sands.

High in the west face of the church tower, above the large window of Perpendicular tracery (which probably replaced unglazed arrow slits in the more peaceful 15th century) there is a *Pieta*, or as others call it, a *Mater dolorosa;* a carving representing the dead Christ, down from the cross and lying across his mother's knees. The Great Urswick example is in red sandstone, most likely taken from Furness Abbey, but now weathered by centuries of western wind and rain almost out of all recognition. The pieta, the Norman doorway on the south side, (still holding remnants of the old 'cow chain', to keep these wandering beasts out of the nave in earlier days) 15th century window-glass holding the armorial bearings of many local families, and the four great bells, all give further proof (if any were needed) of age and long human settlement. The largest bell bears the inscription *Maria Wilelmus de Haryngton Dominus de Aldyngham et Domina Margareta Uxor Eius* which in rough translation means 'William Harrington, Lord of Aldingham, and Lady Margaret his wife ...'. These bells were most likely given originally to Conishead Priory in the 1400s, (Sir William died in 1440) by the Harrington family and came to Urswick in the 16th century after the Dissolution of Conishead Priory. Two other bells were presented by church wardens in 1711 and 1724 respectively. The last bell was presented in 1953, replacing a gap in the row. The original fourth bell, dating at least from the time of Edward VI (he died in 1553) was supposedly stolen by the vicar of Dalton!

If proof were needed of the great age of this site as one of Christian worship, there is a touching monument within the church. On the internal sill of one window, by the door on the south side of the church, is a Saxon gravestone, complete with a dedication by one Tunwini to his lord, cut in crude misshapen Saxon runes. In translation, it reads 'Tunwini erected this in memory of Torhtred, a monument to his lord. Pray for his soul ...'. A further inscription mentions the mason 'Lyl, who wrought this stone ...', and as positive proof of early Saxon Christians here then, the stone has a representation of the Crucifixion on one side, and one of Adam and Eve on the other. This memorial has been dated to about the late 9th century A.D.

Another fragment of stone here speaks of another race which followed and eventually mingled with the Saxon settlers; this is a portion of a former Scandinavian wheel-cross, dated between 950/1000 A.D., put up by Vikings, or Norse-Irishmen. Quite likely, the original cross was carved by a local Saxon craftsman; the Saxon carvers and masons being so much better at these jobs!

Jumping forward a few centuries, into late medieval time, one local lord was standard bearer to Henry V at Agincourt. Indeed, a village tale insists that two local lads, the brothers Fell, sturdy longbowmen, were also there!

Two more of the Harringtons, father and son, were killed at the Battle of Wakefield in 1460, during the Wars of the Roses. Another and later battle is remembered by the title of one of the pubs in the village. There are two of these, the *Derby Arms*, and the *General Burgoyne*. Both are welcoming, friendly typical country pubs. The 'Derby' is named after the former most powerful landowner of the district, the *General Burgoyne* after the English commander soundly defeated at Saratoga, the final battle in the American War of Independence. Burgoyne, as a young man, eloped with Derby's daughter! The *General Burgoyne* pub, the only one of that title anywhere in Britain as far as I can discover, was first so named

The General Burgoyne inn at Urswick and (inset) the general as he appears on the sign. The inn was named by a veteran of the American War of Independence who served with the general

sometime before 1795 by innkeeper Francis Stephenson, who was a giant of a man, 6 feet 2 inches in height and weighing 18 stones. He served for some time as a humble foot soldier in the American War under General Burgoyne.

And what of Little Urswick, the other part? The history here is neither obvious nor blatant. It has 17th and 18th century cottages and houses and a venerable old pub, *The Swan.* Close by is a grammar school founded in Elizabethan days and with one of its first governors a known murderer! (He was Nicolas Bardsey, leader of the mob involved in the Sandys affair of Conishead Priory, in 1558.) There are dark stories of religious persecution here too, when Catholic families (and later, any Quakers) went in fear of their lives. At Bolton Hall, nearby, there are memories of the Stanley family, whose forces turned the tables against Richard III at Bosworth Field in 1485. The sloping green fronting the present building (now a thriving junior school) once held a cockpit, where villagers, teachers, priest and schoolboys all watched each exciting main, or fight, of this bloody sport - held every Shrove Tuesday, of all times! Gentle John Bolton also lived nearby; a humble villager turned fossil expert whose advice, early last century, was sought by many of the high and mighty in this field.

Urswick Tarn, between Little and Great Urswick, is very rich in wildlife. Birds include great crested grebes, sedge warblers in season, green woodpecker and the occasional rare kingfisher as well as the common host of mallard and coot (an Urswick villager today is still proud to be called an "Ossick coot", and there is a Coot Restaurant here, right by the water). Cormorants fish for eels, tufted duck dive for zebra mussels, water rails stalk the reed beds, and parson-collared reed buntings nest in them. Trolius, the lovely buttercup-yellow globe flower grows here together with the loveliest of all geraniums, the 'Mourning Widow', the Dusky Cranesbill; a garden escapee rapidly approaching naturalisation and admittance to the British wild flower list.

At the tarn outflow, where the water begins its short race to the sea, blunt-nosed water voles burrow in the red earth of the bank. Pike, carp, perch, tench and the aforementioned eels of all sizes thrive in this water, together with the giant swan mussel, *Anodon cygneus*, some of these large shellfish 'weighing more than 9

Giant Swan Mussel, Anodon Cygneus, *from Urswick Tarn*

ounces each ...' according to one writer. Each of these freshwater mussels is enclosed in a tough shell coloured a dirty black-brown but inside, each has a coating of glorious rainbow-hued mother-of-pearl! The two Urswicks, in history and natural history, are hard to equal anywhere in Furness, but there are some rivals.

Another village steeped in history, for example, and not far away to the west, is Gleaston. This is the Saxon 'farm by the smooth river', and, indeed, it is built above the flood plain of Gleaston Beck, another misfit stream of a flat-bottomed former meltwater channel. Like Urswick, the older Gleaston houses are of limestone, but here there is a difference. Look at the barn wall at the west end of the village street (by the signpost, set in an old millstone), or at the former pound at the east end of the village, now a neat little allotment. This is a near-circular enclosure, once holding cattle impounded for straying, the owners being fined a fixed sum per animal. Amongst the limestone boulders of the pound, and those of the barn, there are slabs of dark rock, almost purple in colour and obviously not the native limestone.This dark stone is *dolerite,* an abyssal volcanic rock occurring originally as dykes or sills of molten material intruded into the native rock millions of years ago; it is the same material of which the Whin Sill is made, the steel-hard stone which carries the Roman Wall of Hadrian on its dark-tinted back, and ends up in the North Sea as the craggy black scatter known as the Farne Islands. Dolerite, closely allied to basalt, is from the Greek 'doleros' - 'difficult' - for it is difficult to place amongst rock types. In tiny Gleaston, it is scattered throughout the village.

Gleaston Mill, less than a quarter of a mile north-east of the village proper, was in use within the last 30 years but is now no longer working. It was a breast mill, with the water led half a mile through the fields onto the wheel buckets towards the top, turning the huge, metal-framed wheel anti-clockwise. The wheel, mill machinery, and mill gearing (these last made from pear-wood, the miller told me, years ago) lie idle; but there is hope. The iron-framed wheel is restored and refitted with new oaken buckets and the leat, the water channel, cleaned and cleared. With a lot of work and even more money, it is hoped that the mill will be working once more in the not too distant future. This was once a 'king's mill', owned in turn by Henry VIII, the first Elizabeth, and James I, the canny Scot - who promptly sold it. I suggest that a mill of sorts has been here for centuries. Perhaps it was here in the 13th and 14th centuries; or even earlier, in Saxon times. The early English were great bread eaters and skilled millers; this village was and still is surrounded by excellent corn-growing, arable land.

Half a mile beyond the mill is Gleaston Castle, a badly neglected

The ruins of Gleaston Castle. Too little and too late, it was soon abandoned

limestone ruin. It was the seat of the Harrington family already mentioned, who by various family marriages, became the owners of the le Fleming property. The family progression from that first motte and bailey on the shore of Aldingham to Gleaston Castle, several miles inland, probably took a couple of centuries.

The date of the building of Gleaston Castle is not known, but it was some time after the disastrous Bruce raid of 1322. Then, as with so many things in Britain, Gleaston Castle, built as a stronghold against further Scots invasion, came too little and too late. It was built in a hurry, as a glance at the western wall will show. Here the mortared outer fabric has gone, revealing a rubble infill; not cemented, or mortared, but packed in simple, unworked clay! The last owners, the Harrington, were never happy with the castle; indeed by the mid-15th century it was abandoned and already on the way to ruin.

It is a strange place, haunted by pale-eyed jackdaws and the occasional kestrel; massive fireplaces and crumbling stairways remain, with arrow-slit windows and circular stairs, but all of it now unsafe. There is no massive central keep as is usual with this castle-pattern; there never was. Nor is there any evidence of violence done here, nor of siege, nor battle. Gleaston Castle is a badly designed fortress, hurriedly constructed and obsolete almost as soon as completed. For one thing, it appears to have no self-contained water-supply and for another, longbowmen standing on the top of a nearby drumlin, could fire almost at will into the space enclosed by the castle. Briefly, Gleaston Castle may have been no more than a draughty, damp castle-cum-little-used-country-seat of the Harringtons which, generally neglected by them, was soon abandoned.

Outside the castle walls the area is well endowed with pure, ice-cold springs of freshwater, but some of their surroundings are cattle-poached, messy and difficult to investigate. Brooklime, a bright blue and beautiful bloom with a pronounced affinity for lime-rich habitat, flowers in the becks alongside. On the walls of the south-eastern tower (with masonry still nearly 30 feet high) are scores of small, bright-red stemmed plants, sprouting from cracks in the stonework or between the blocks of masonry. This is *Parietaria judaica*, Pellitory-of-the-Wall, closely related to the common nettle. In medieval times and later it was grown as a useful medicinal plant to cure bladder troubles, kidney stones, coughs, burns and general inflammation! It is uncommon in the district, which makes one wonder if it be an escapee from some lost Gleaston Castle herb garden of long ago? Close by there is an old and neglected quarry from which the tough limestone blocks of the castle were hewn; it is rich in fossils of the Carboniferous era. Further along the road south, back towards the village by yet another bubbling spring, there is an ancient limekiln.

The road north from the castle leads to Scales, once another centre of Quaker activity. Before that place, there is yet another *dub*, or hollow holding a small stretch of water. Called Mere Tarn, shallow and reed-fringed, it is rich in birdlife throughout the year. It may have its own attendant flock of feral greylag geese or teal resting on the water. Pintail, perhaps the fastest flying duck on the British list, visit here, while coot, moorhen, mallard, heron, little grebes, and mute swan are common. Two years ago it was a winter roost of thousands of starlings, and at the same time, the hedges

Mere Tarn, Gleaston, once used by the villagers in flax preparation and now the home of unusual birds. The tarn is a typical 'kettle' left by the ice age

alongside held hundreds of fieldfares and redwings.

In the 17th century, the pool was used for 'retting' flax, a preparation in making linen; a method which includes immersing the stalks in water until the outer covering rots away. The channels in which this was done may be seen today at the forefront of the encroaching reed beds. When water was very short during one 17th century drought, the villagers of Gleaston and Scales quarrelled violently over who was to take drinking water from the tarn!

Scales, a hamlet of pure Norse name barely a mile from Gleaston Castle, is a tiny farming complex with old, 17th century houses, (one with a massive, recently rediscovered inglenook, another with the delightful name of Cheesepress). Probably it was first settled as an outlier of the richer Gleaston land held by the Saxons.

Leece, another village nearer Barrow, apart from the increasing number of modern houses, is somewhat similar, complete with village green, duck pond and modern equivalent of village blacksmith - but no 'spreading chestnut tree'! It was once a grange of Furness Abbey monks and contains a scatter of 17th and 18th century cottages and old farms. Another hamlet recorded as 'Little Lees' in the early Middle Ages was located nearby, but

Newton where there was a bloody Civil War skirmish

it has gone long since without leaving the tiniest trace.

Newton, a small village close by the Abbey itself, is a small collection of houses where a nasty, bloody, Civil War skirmish took place. For once, in a strongly Roundhead area, the Royalists temporarily got the better of the Cromwellian forces. The Parliamentary fleet was moored by Piel as an Irish invasion was suspected, the over-confident soldiers investing and enjoying Newton village. Surprised by the Royalists, many retreated to the pound at the western entrance to the village. The site of this is now covered by modern bungalows. Though part of the old pound wall bordering the field is still recognisable. Here, any Roundheads fighting within it were 'killed or taken', as a cold-blooded account has it. Those fleeing to Piel harbour were attacked savagely all the way, 'even to the very side of their ships'. It was not a battle but a scuffle - a dirty, bloody business as often happens in any war. Most of the older Newton village houses are now modernised out of recognition; number 30, however (now called White Rose Cottage) has a massive indoor fireplace and a rediscovered inglenook in a magnificent chimney dating, I suspect, from the early 17th century or even the late 16th. Chiselled sandstone 'Padstones' were discovered along the base of one inner wall, where normally in this type of house there are suitable unworked boulders forming wall foundations. I suspect that this sandstone masonry was 'quarried' - stolen - from Furness Abbey soon after the Dissolution of 1537 by a quick-witted villager seizing his chance! There can be no doubt that this house is ancient; indeed, it was altered in the mid-18th century, according to the deeds, and was old even then! The older houses in these Cumbrian villages rarely date back beyond the 17th century, for this was the time when the earlier farms and cottages - probably thatched huts of turf and timber - were replaced by those built in stone. It was a time of improving agriculture, of growing enrichment for many, so that most of the more ancient farming hovels were swept away for ever.

Stainton, the 'stony settlement' lies barely a mile east of Newton, the 'New' farm. It existed as a human settlement long before Abbey monks arrived and made Newton their grange. Stainton, as a settlement site, is very old indeed; intensive quarrying early this century blasted away an Iron Age village here; a place of long standing, where, amongst other things, snail shells, found by the barrowload, proved wholesale use of these molluscs as food by these ancient villagers. The mass of shells was discovered amongst the remains and relics of stone-based huts. Now all are gone, but 17th century Stainton Hall remains. It was once owned by a branch of the Washington family which produced the first President of the United States. On the west end of the village green, the Hall may be recognised instantly by the huge chimney. The green itself still bears the firm trace of a cockpit ring; one used by former villagers and visitors from far and wide, almost within living memory. Stainton was and still is a quarrying village; the massive stones in some of the field walls bear evidence to the skill - and strength - of former villagers!

Dendron, tucked in a tiny valley away from all of these bigger places, is a minuscule hamlet of perhaps five or six houses and farms, plus a lovely little church. Not much there, unless you pay a visit in early spring when rooks caw in the branches of tall, undiseased elms and the odd but attractive little church seems to float first on a sea of snowdrops and soon afterwards, on a breathtaking tide of purple, chrome-yellow, and bleach-white crocus. You can also see the cow backscratcher in the field to the south. This curiosity is no more than a rough slab of limestone of a type invented, so they say, by a past Duke of Argyll, for the relief of cattle with itchy back or side! 'God bless the Duke of Argyle', the cows are supposed to say, every time (which means often!) they scratch back luxuriously against these tall and suitably roughened limestone pillars!

What other villages are there in Low Furness? There is Lindal, between Dalton and Ulverston, which is in two halves. As part of a class conscious Victorian tradition, Lindal has stone-built houses, presumably put up for the former administrators of the mines which made this place both rich and busy. These are built carefully around the present village green. Much of the other half of the village, built for railway workers as well as miners, lies across the A590, the main Ulverston/Barrow road which cuts the place in two. More cottages line the main road, again the former houses of humbler mine or railway employees. The two main jobs in the Lindal of yesteryear were mining and the railway. One fed the other. Lindal iron-ore was shunted and assembled in wagons at Lindal junction which in its heyday was very important and very busy. Now, it has gone completely; there is no station and all tracks leading in and out of the former loading complex were pulled up long ago. No railway lines other than the twin track of the main line between Carnforth and Barrow remain.

Lindal village green was once a tarn with water the colour of blood due to washing crimson-stained carts used to ferry haematite down to Barrow. (These carts had girl drivers when the supply of boys ran out!) The tarn was filled-in long ago. The mines are gone, the village little more than a dormitory with two farms still working. One is Church Farm, an ivy-covered, 17th century building which formerly belonged to Greenwich Hospital, which supports the Chelsea pensioners.

Lindal achieved brief fame, or notoriety, in late Victorian times, when it

Lindal village green was once a tarn where ore carts were washed, turning the water blood red

lost a complete steam locomotive. It vanished when the line holding it was swallowed up by sudden mine subsidence, though fortunately there was time for the driver and fireman to jump clear. All efforts were made to recover the Lindal engine, but it sank determinedly and swiftly out of sight. It is still there, entombed in bright red-brown clay, and probably many feet down below the surface by now.

Two more villages of Low Furness spring to mind. One is Ireleth, just over the hill from Lindal and at the seaward end of the 1763 Kendal/Ireleth turnpike. *Ireleth* means the hill slope of the Irish, and the name is very old. Which Irish? Could it be those Norse Irish again, whose place-names crop up time and time again on the western seaboard of the county? Possibly some of the refugees already mentioned, fleeing here from across the Irish Sea to escape the wrath of a Viking king? If so, then it is a chilling thought that the original inhabitants of Ireleth may well have been former Viking slavers! Dublin was a busy and highly profitable slave-market, known throughout western Europe in the 10th century A.D.; it was also a long established Norse settlement. Some of the former Dubliners coming here (if indeed they were from that city) may well have been involved in slave-trading! An interesting thought - but, unfortunately, one without any

Fisher Quarry at Kirkby - a vast slate quarry, still in use

record or proof, or even hint, other than reasoned speculation of it being true. One later school of thought includes Gaels in the Norse influx into Cumbria, second generation Gaelic-Norsemen coming from Galloway, and the Western Isles. Even so, there seems to be a strong connection between the Norsemen of Ireland and Cumbria in the very late 10th and equally early 11th centuries.

Last on my list of Low Furness villages is Kirkby, which is really three separate settlements. There is Sandside, which grew up first about the ford over Duddon Sands, and shipped Kirkby slate in bulky flatts, the common coastal ship-type of the time used on these low, tidal shores. The hostelry where travellers drank before or after crossing the hazardous Duddon

Sands is still there. This is *The Ship*, a 17th century pub opposite a barn* carved with the names of the giant horses used in the slate quarries up on the edge of the moor, as well as those of the mighty visiting stallions which bred them. Sandside holds 17th century cottages, and grew from a fishing settlement and host to over-sand travellers. The arrival of the railway helped it grow even more, for it took over the transport of slate, and the quarries thrived.

A mile down the road is Marshside, a hamlet once devoted to slate quarrying, and much younger than Sandside. Across the main road is Kirkby Hall, once the seat of the family of that name, but one ruined completely by the Civil War. It has thick stone walls, massive round chimneys, and suitably enough for a strongly Royalist Catholic family, its own decorated and rather secretive chapel. Kirkby Hall, also known as Cross House from the ancient preaching cross stationed by the front door, is very old indeed, it reeks of history. It was the home of the Kirkbys, an ancient family who ruined themselves (and lost sons) in supporting the king during the Civil War. The Hall is now a private farm, but well worth a visit.

The third section of Kirkby is the linear village of Beckside which, as its name implies, it is on the edge of a stream. The stream rushes down from the western slopes of Kirkby Moor, under which the village seems to crouch. This is a very old settlement, the present church having Norman features but on a site which is much older than those arrogant invaders. The full name is Kirkby Ireleth and as suggested elsewhere in the book, is a Norse Irish inversion, this form of place-name proving the existence of a church here long before the Normans arrived. Beckside has the remains of an old corn mill but the village is little more than one delightful old street at the bottom of a very steep road from Ulverston, coming down from a windswept and almost barren moor. Upstream, there are some delightful waterfalls whilst on the moor there is the chance of seeing red grouse and ravens, kestrel hawk or peregrine, glorious emperor moths or green hairstreak butterflies, flitting over banks of purple heather and whitening stands of tough, sheep-proof nardus grass.

Indeed, as I have tried to show, the villages of Low Furness are as varied and as different as the topography of Furness itself. Histories, lifestyles, architecture and appearance show great variety; far more than ever be revealed in this book. Personal investigation and exploration is the key; plus patience, for though there is much to discover, most is revealed only to those who take care to explore and investigate.

*The barn is now a private house.

7: Wordsworth's Valley

THE DUDDON ESTUARY, the entry of the River Duddon (reputedly Wordsworth's favourite river) to the sea, gapes wide at its final meeting with the tides. Across the northern skyline, over the braided channels at low water, or the sparkling tide at full, the Lakeland mountains dominate the river's entry to the sea. For our purpose, the journey begins on the southern bank, beyond the tawny dunes of Sandscale and by a large village with its feet in sea-sand. The place is Askam; a bright Victorian hope at one time; formerly sitting on a buried mountain of high grade haematite and at a time when the nation was crying out for more and yet more iron and steel.

That bright hope has long gone; the iron mines are extinct, the old workings flooded and collapsed and though millions of tons of the blood-red ore lie yet untouched beneath the broad estuary, the cost of its recovery is too high in modern terms. Askam-in-Furness was once a bustling, thriving iron-working town, as well as one with profitable mines almost underfoot; the Victorian grid-iron pattern of houses is plain to see, the terraced streets, the friendly pubs giving the town a modern nickname, from the TV soap opera, of 'Coronation Street by the Sea'. Now, inevitably, the developers are moving in; already there is talk of creating a huge shoreside marina.

A long and rocky embankment thrusts out into the estuary; a quay of man-made rock; not concrete, but slag, the cooled remains of the ironwork's once-molten rubbish. There were plans in the mid-19th century to make a sturdy, sea-proof bridge of the slagbank by carrying it across Duddon Sands, with, perhaps, the waste slag from the Millom ironworks over on the Cumberland side extended in another long bank to meet it. Unfortunately, when the railway lines first crept north, the projected west coast route, suggested as a main line, lost out to the eastern proposal, which eventually carried the railway by way of Lancaster and Shap to Carlisle. The ambitious plan to bridge Duddon Sands, like a similar proposal for a viaduct crossing Morecambe Bay, was quietly shelved and eventually, forgotten.

Askam, a Victorian relic, has its charm along the beach. Where an old iron-ore mine tip sprawls down onto the sand, a half-buried spring leaks fresh water into a bed of wild orchids. Several species, and their many hybrids, thrust forth from the thin, wet soil here every late spring and summer in a flare of pink, white and magenta. Early purples, beautiful in form and shape, but smelling of tomcats, are the first of these exotics to appear. These Shakespearean 'Long purples' sprout from the grey and pink face of Roanhead Crags, along the beach; sad reminders of Hamlet's poor drowned Ophelia:

There with fantastic garlands
did she come,
Of crow flowers, nettles,
daisies and Long purples
That liberal shepherds gave
a grosser name,
But our cold maids do dead
men's fingers call them ...

Later in the season, purple, white and yellow flowers of heart's ease, tiny dune pansies, brighten the sand beyond the blue-green lances of tall sea lyme grass. Sea-holly shows vivid blue flowers against grey-blue spined and spiky leaves, alongside brightest emerald-green Portland spurge, charming, milky-juiced, and poisonous! Centaury shows shell-pink spires in the turf, while long-stemmed field pansies appear in chrome and lemon yellow bursts of bloom beneath the long needles of marram grass, growing directly from the gritty sand. Feathery-leaved tufts of lousewort appear in the damper patches, beyond the foredunes, where sea-twitch, tough relative of the toughest of grasses, strives hard not to be buried in wind-drifted sand. The uncommon Isle of Man cabbage grows hard by the slagbank, and on that dusty pile, the tufted purple of fleabane and the fleshy, yellow-flowered cushions of wall pepper, better known as stonecrop, spread over this volcanic-like dry soil. Askam beach, and its overgrown and forgotten industrial relics, is a botanist's summer paradise.

Along the long, long beach, by salty tidal pools full of wriggling mosquito larvae, the rare natterjacks occasionally emerge in summer dusk to feed. Here, rearing abruptly from the sand, is the hump of Dunnerholme, a grey limestone outcrop. Millions of years ago, even before the coal measures formed, it was a coral reef, growing in warm and sunlit shallow seas of some unknown tropic. Fossil coral appears in the grey white stone as relics of that ancient time and in parts the rock is tinted with the blush of haematite, or the rusty shades of another iron oxide, limonite. Now the outcrop fringes marshland hiding a bay on its northern flank where winter wildfowl, pintail, shoveller, wigeon, mallard and merganser may shelter by the thousand when tide and wind are high together. Dunnerholme is a fossil reef, but one well endowed by other fossils; great spiral shells and smaller molluscs, embedded in sea-smoothed rock. This outcrop was an easy source of limestone, quarried not so long ago so that the island is hollow. It was taken and burnt on site to provide lime for plaster and for fertilizer, scattered as a white powder to sweeten acid and unproductive soil. There are three defunct and crumbling limekilns built into the cliffs on the north side, relics of a once-busy localised industry. Quarried Dunnerholme stone, well broken, was also added to iron-ore in the furnace by Duddon Bridge, to remove impurities, and be in turn tapped off as useless, molten slag.

A short row of cottages, formerly owned by cockle-fishermen (for Duddon Sand shellfish were famous in the north, even in Elizabethan days) huddle under Dunnerholme's eastern lee. Across the flat fields, half a mile away, Marsh Grange, a tall and rather lordly farm, seems strangely out of place in such windswept flattened land. Marsh Grange, as the name suggests, *was* once a grange, an outlying farm, belonging to Furness Abbey. Theirs from the early 12th to the Dissolution of 1537, it was farmed and cultivated, drained and cleared by hardworking peasants in charge of an appointed lay brother belonging to the Abbey. In the 17th century, it was the home of Margaret Askew, the same Margaret who at 17, became Margaret Fell, wife of Judge Fell, of Swarthmoor Hall, was widowed, married George Fox, and earned her title of Mother of the Quakers by many years of indomitable faith and courage against her determined and bigoted religious persecutors.

Beyond Marsh Grange, the coast is rather flat and uninteresting, though it does have a fine show of wildfowl in the winter. It borders an ancient moss of Angerton; a lovely miniature wilderness of old peat diggings, where birch and Scots pine, rowan, bracken and willow struggle to clothe and cover the land; a place where the ground underfoot quakes and heaves with every step. Many local people above the moss still retain turbary rights on their own section of Angerton Moss. This is the legal right, often dating back centuries, to cut peat for winter fuel. Nowadays, few seem to bother, and the moss, now being drained, is still rich in wildlife and a rather lonely place in winter. In the time of the Abbey, some of the peat cut here was taken by people living as far afield as Biggar Village, on Walney; indeed, the old peat-carters' road across the marsh south of Sandscale and Roanhead dunes is still in existence, but ignored and unnoticed by the many. Angerton Moss is perhaps one of the few last wildernesses in all Cumbria where the six-foot-high royal fern *Osmunda regalis* (which got its name by hiding a Saxon King Osmund from his assassins) flourishes close by cotton flags, great sprawls of tall, spear-like reeds, bulrush and giant tufts of purple moorgrass. Where also the creeping plants and crimson, tart, fruit of cranberries lies cushioned in huge green mounts of sphagnum moss.

Angerton is a place with its own crumbling and disused 17th century farm, a blessed sanctuary for resident foxes, badgers, kingfishers and, some say, hen harriers, scarce, long legged avian predators of marshland and waving reed bed.

The moss, former estuary to Torver Beck and marking where it spilt out into the sea, gives way to Foxfield which is now not much more than a railway halt on the west coast line. Once, Foxfield was the junction for the Coniston line, until the heavy hand of Dr Beeching swept away the Coniston track for ever. After Foxfield and gradually, past the tiny hamlet of Greety Gate (which means stony road, a former ford over the Duddon river), the estuary begins to narrow into the River Duddon proper. Nearby, at the so-called 'Donkey Rocks' - which some call the 'Frozen River' - there is a quarry of soft red shale. This is perhaps the fossilized tail-end of a turbidity current, where silt and natural rubbish, eroded many million of years ago by a fast-flowing river from a long-gone, unknown continent, spread the silt into giant, undersea mounds with steeper and steeper slope. Eventually, the whole mass slid down into the ocean depths at a furious speed, an undersea, gigantic tumble of mud and rock. Now, heaved up from the sea, frozen by time, it retains, within the red shale, the rounded boulders and cobbles carried along in each powerful submarine avalanche of so very long ago.

The estuary narrows rapidly, the true river running between recognisable banks becoming more and more obvious. Hemmed in on the west, the lower side, by a levee, a raised green bank, the Duddon narrows, and soon on the eroding right bank, the crumbling remains of an old wharf appear, backed by a once well-paved road. This was farthest point up river where bulky, wide-beamed sailing flatts, little more than barges, discharged the red Furness iron-ore, haematite, to be taken by horse and cart along the riverside track to a charcoal iron furnace, beyond Duddon Bridge, where, before the merging of the counties in 1974, the main road crossed over from North Lancashire to Cumberland.

Duddon Bridge Furnace, much of it still standing as a remarkable industrial relic, is properly beyond the scope of a book devoted to 'Lost Lancashire'. Until 1974 it lay in old Cumberland, on the true right bank of the river; the Duddon being the time-honoured boundary between these two counties. Lancashire ended on the left bank, the river being the natural boundary between the two counties. Yet it would be a pity not to mention this unique 18th century furnace, the finest of its kind in the country. The whole site is being cleared and cleaned; and there was even talk of getting

Ruined offices of the Duddon Bridge Furnace
(see also colour illustration of the furnace)

it into production again, occasionally, for the tourist trade, which would make it a marvellous attraction. Unfortunately, the cost of such an enterprise is much too high. At present, the furnace is being cleared of undergrowth, with paths and buildings being restored where possible. Information boards show it as a fine example of early 18th century charcoal-iron making, dating from the early years of the Industrial Revolution.

In 1736, it was reported that '... Mr Hall and Company are already begun to erect a new Furness *(sic)* and other Commodious buildings at Dudden Bridge ...'. It was to work almost without any change of method, for a further 130 years until 1867 when it finally ceased. The iron-ore for the furnace came by barge from several mines near the Dalton and Lindal of Low Furness. The charcoal - always in short supply, for the making of it was slow and laborious - was made as near to site as possible in the Duddon Woods, as the surrounding trees, still bearing traces of coppicing, bear witness. The furnace made pig-iron, in which molten iron was tapped from the furnace base into beds of firm moulding sand (the resulting pattern resembled a pig suckling its young). A huge wheel, driven by River Duddon water, worked giant bellows to keep the charcoal and ore at white heat, fusing the metal, but burning off the impurities into slag. Unfortunately, work there was generally intermittent; more often interrupted by shortages of charcoal but sometimes, when the river was low during drought, by insufficient water to work the all-important wheel.

This unique furnace site could certainly be visited, but it is better to obtain permission from the Lake District Planning Board at Kendal beforehand. It is best seen in winter when much of the surrounding tree foliage is down. Seen in February, the entrance to the old works is white with drifts of snowdrops, which grow here completely wild. Later on, bluebells and wood anemones take over, and the banks of beck and field drain show the bright green and sulphur cushions of golden saxifrage.

The true left bank of the River Duddon - or the right bank looking upstream - is the former Lancashire side. It is best approached by way of Broughton-in-Furness, little more than a mile to the south-east. A delightful little village, with a charming square modelled on that of an 18th century London site, it has a central stone pillar memorial, slabs from which fresh fish (flounders and cockles from the estuary, salmon and trout from the Duddon) were once sold and old wooden stocks. Two of the pubs, the *Black Cock*, and the *King's Head* are oak-beamed, very old, and with friendly host and staff. The church, below the village, is set in a sea of soft grass, the fabric about the tower containing huge stones which are probably Saxon work. This building is very old - or rather parts of it are - for unfortunately, like so many English churches, it is very much Victorianised. It lies on flatter land and at one time, before the advent of the railway which changed much of the coastline, it would have had feet in the sea!

The road north and west, out of Broughton, via the *High Cross Inn*, high on a hill, swoops down towards Duddon Bridge, the widened 18th century structure still a nightmare for the careless motorist. However, the road we take turns off before this, and leads steeply uphill within a few hundred yards. By

The wharf on the Duddon where ore was unloaded and iron shipped out

The Square, Broughton in Furness, with stocks and fish slabs

way of woods, old farms, and a noisy cattle-grid, it leads out into unfenced stretches of open, steeply sloping, bracken-clad fell. The river is far below, to the left; on the right, bare hillsides sweep up to a rocky skyline. The road then begins to fall again, and fall is the operative word, for it drops down steeply towards the wind of the river, unfenced and unguarded, where sheep are likely to treat passing traffic with the utmost contempt. To the right, winding up a dry gorge, is an old fell road, beautifully made, but rather like a miniature, greener Khyber Pass. This is the Priest's Road, built, supposedly, for a busy parish priest of long ago. More likely, it was made to serve the packhorse trade, where mules brought iron-ore to medieval bloomeries scattered about these open hillsides, always sited by water of some kind.

A mile further on, after yet more ups and down on the narrow road, one arrives at Ulpha, by a former packhorse bridge which though widened, is still an awkward, narrow span to negotiate by car. This was the passage into Cumberland before 1974, and over this narrow bridge, until early in the 19th century, herds of black Irish cattle came down from the old drove road crossing the northern fells. They were driven from the fattening grazing fields of Bootle, or the quayside at Whitehaven, the drovers seeking markets at busy Broughton, or Ulverston; or they were taken further, crossing the treacherous Morecambe Bay sands to Lancaster, Preston and the south.

This cattle trade was very important in the economy of the region, so one may imagine the panic in the mid-18th century when a certain murrain, or cattle plague (most likely foot and mouth disease, less possibly rinderpest or the terrible anthrax) broke out in force in Cumberland. Immediately, a watch was set on all bridges crossing the Duddon, and to prevent possible spread of the murrain no Cumberland cattle, or their drovers, were allowed entry into Lancashire. A stone, set up on Ulpha bridge by these sentries of

Ulpha bridge, ancient boundary between Lancashire and Cumberland

long ago marked the occasion. Cut deeply into the rock is the word *Watch* and the date, *1749*. This stone was here until 1985, when it disappeared in mysterious fashion, most probably taken by vandals or thieves. Two more bridges which crossed the Duddon from Cumberland and still existing, are Cockley Beck, at the head of the dale and Duddon Bridge, at its foot. Though both are likely contemporaries of the 1749 Ulpha bridge, no trace of any similar carving can be found on them today, despite careful search.

Immediately downstream from Ulpha bridge, the hurrying river slows and opens out into deep, silent, and turquoise-tinted pools. By the bridge the road crosses over to the old Cumberland side, by noisy river rapids and a row of tall black pines, (planted to celebrate Queen Victoria's Diamond Jubilee?) Here is the tiny Ulpha church. This too was a place which like the whole valley, was once much loved by Wordsworth:

The Kirk of Ulpha to the pilgrim's eye
Is Welcome as a star, that doth present
Is shining forehead through the peaceful rent
Of a black cloud diffus'd o'er half the sky ...

he wrote, of this simple dale church beside the rushing river.

The grey road, still narrow, still wriggling about the valley like some giant snake, next heads for Seathwaite; on the right bank here, we are still in old Cumberland, but shortly before Seathwaite, the road crosses the Duddon once again, back into pre-1974 Lancashire. This modern bridge is at Hall Dunnerdale, a place-name revealing ancient origins. For Hall Dunnerdale is a title written back-to-front - yet another of those fascinating place-name inversions scattered like confetti about the western flanks of Cumbria.

Yet Hall Dunnerdale, despite its seemingly impressive title, is little more than a couple of farms and a tiny cluster of cottages. On the right bank of the river, in front of one house, the outline of a huge fish is cut into slate slabs topping the low wall, close by steps where the people here once drew water from the river. The original fish of this crude outline carving was a true giant, a salmon caught here in 1933 by the occupant of the house close by. He laid it out on the slabs immediately, and first drew, and then cut around the body shape; some say by using a six-inch nail as chisel. This was carefully performed both to give a permanent record of the size and the shape of the huge fish, and at the same time prevent the proud fisherman from a charge of boasting!

Seathwaite, the *thveit* or clearing of the *saetr* the upland summer grazing field of some long dead Viking, is also a very tiny place. It contains a pub, a barn converted to holiday flats, a vicarage, and a simple Victorian church which replaced the former chapel, once the domain of Robert Walker. He was a remarkable man and marvellous priest, an incumbent here from 1735 to 1802. His largest stipend reached £40, but he started as curate of Seathwaite, at the age of 26, on £5 a year! He taught children, using the church as schoolroom, became a classical scholar, grew his own food on glebe land, sheared his own sheep (taking the wool on his back to Broughton market, seven miles away over the fells, in all weathers), spun, wove blankets and cloth, tanned the hides of his own cattle for shoe leather, and helped all his neighbours with their harvesting and sheep-shearing. On top of all this he was doctor to the parish, clerk and letter-writer for the illiterate, a brewer of beer, and writer of all the legal documents for his less educated parishioners. He reared a family of eight while his salary was no more than £20, kept open house for all, and left the then vast sum of more than £2,000 to his sorrowing folk when he died at the age of 93. He has been discussed and written about almost *ad nauseum*, but it should be remembered that there were several Lakeland parsons not unlike him busy in his own day and age.

Seathwaite, of all places, was the scene of a riot one fine summer day in July, 1904. Navvies, newly paid, (it was "Pay Monday", the pay-day) who had been working on the sea wall at Haverigg, walked over from Millom. Although this is a long way, some were tipsy before they started! They met other navvies in Seathwaite, mostly Irishmen hired to build a reservoir and dam high up on the fells above Seathwaite, a catchment area for Barrow Water Works. Some of the Haverigg men, quarrelsome in drink, got out of hand, besieging the *Newfield Inn*, after first being thrown out for wrecking it. The frightened landlord, barman and an engineer of the Water Works barricaded themselves in the pub and armed with shotguns, faced a crowd throwing lumps of wood and heavy scraps of iron, together with wall cobbles and stones dug from the road. A few, far gone in excitement and drink, were screaming for murder! Inevitably, one poor drunk, John Kavanagh, was shot by one of those defending the battered pub and died that night from his wounds. Joseph Foy, another drunken navvy was also shot, and lost a leg because of it - which is not surprising, for after primary treatment and suffering from extensive loss of blood, he was carried in a jolting, bumping cart over the terrible valley roads to Ulverston, 11 miles away, to receive further medical attention! Meanwhile, 20 policemen had arrived to quell the riot, together with the Broughton doctor, summoned to treat the wounded men. By then it was all over, the shaken crowd dispersed, a few clearing up the mess. As well as interior loss and damage the *Newfield Inn* had 42 panes of glass broken, while the vicarage, school and church, showing the mindlessness of the crowd, had a total of 102 window panes smashed to smithereens. There are no reminders of the riot here now; the church and churchyard are serene and near-silent places, the simple chair made by the ever-active Walker, the stone on which he straddled his Herdwick sheep for clipping and his simple gravestone slab in the churchyard, are all there still.

Opposite the church, a footpath leads through woodland and across the fields to the farm of High Wallabarrow, a typical fell farm tucked under the huge, castle-like cliff of Wallabarrow Crag, towering 600 feet above. The narrowing river is spanned by a modern stone footbridge, below which are stepping-stones, reputedly used and named by Wordsworth. The woodland itself is birch and hazel, with a few scattered oak standards. In May, the wood floor is a sea of bluebells, over which the buzzards spiral and mew like lost kittens. It is a lovely place, with wood warblers singing here every spring and summer, and the green woodpeckers calling against curlew nesting higher up the valley slopes.

After climbing up and away from Seathwaite, and with many more twists and turns, the valley eventually flattens out into a wide dalehead. On the way there, the road passes Birk's Bridge, a narrow, low-parapeted arch of stone, built for packhorses carrying goods to and from the coast; many of the loads, according to local legend, smuggled in at dead of night from ships standing offshore. Goods like silks, salt, tobacco and brandy. Indeed, anything which was charged by the Inland Revenue found a ready market when brought over the Cumbrian coast from the 'Smuggler's Warehouse', or the 'Warehouse of Frauds' as the Isle of Man was then called.

Birk's Bridge is beautiful in any season; a delightful grey arch over deep, still pools the colour of copper-sulphate solution. In autumn, the fiery berries of rowan trees glow like so many lamps against the grey and rocky river bank. Behind them, beyond the water, there are acres of tall and silent spruces, western red cedars and Scots pine, with a multitude of tracks and trails running through them like so many rabbit runs. This is the summer haunt of pied flycatchers and the darting 'firetails', the lovely redstarts.

At Cockley Beck, usually regarded as the dalehead, the road divides. One way travels to Eskdale; the road crosses the river by another old bridge and heads due west, up towards the summit of Hard Knott. This mountain pass over into Eskdale is one which holds perhaps the steepest section of road in all England, with a gradient of one in three - but which many swear is nearer one in two! The other way, still keeping to the bounds of old North Lancashire, swings to the right past Cockley Beck Farm, the road leading to another mountain pass which also rears up abruptly from the valley floor, but not quite so steeply as the trial of Hard Knott. This is Wrynose, supposedly the Norseman's 'Pass of the Stallion'; it is from *Reinshals;* a true Norse name as one would expect in this predominantly Viking area. These dalesmen of old are supposed to have said that one needed a good stallion to conquer the high pass and in their day it was probably true.

The modern road, metalled only in post-war years, follows a Roman road for much of the way. This was the track which led from Agricola's supply port of Glanaventa, (modern Ravenglass), used as military supply depot when he invaded Scotland in 82 A.D. The Roman road led straight across country to Galava, close by modern Ambleside, from which place spread a whole network of Roman roads. Approaching Wrynose from Cockley Beck, part of the Roman road stands clear of the modern highway, though its cobbles and paving are hard to trace. It passes by a ruined farm, Gaitscalegarth, where until ruined by a bitter winter a century and more ago, a fell farmer somehow wrested a living from this unyielding, barren land. A severe storm is said to have destroyed 140 of his sheep and the poor man, after that, found it impossible to carry on. The Gaitscalegarth sheep were supposedly different - with one pair of ribs more than any other breed!

The one outstanding man-made features beyond the ruins and on top of

Wrynose Pass, is the Three Shire Stone, a crudely shaped pillar. This slab of limestone, bearing *W.F. 1816* on one side and *Lancashire* on the other, replaced three ancient boundary stones more than a hundred years ago. These old markers were collectively known as the 'three foot brandreth'; a trio of boulders which marked the meeting point of Lancashire, Westmorland and Cumberland. The word *brandreth* was the name for a three-legged Norse stool; a similar marker was found beside the River Lune, at Tebay, in east Westmorland. The Wrynose stones are marked as such a brandreth as early as 1610, on Saxton's map, the earliest dated map of old Westmorland. Cockley Beck, the farm far below to the west, holds deeds mentioning, amongst other things '... the boundary marks of the ancient mannour (manor) of Cockley Beck', obviously meaning the old brandreth stones. They were there in 1692, near the spring which is the source of the River Duddon and are mentioned again in 1777 as 'being three little stones ... about a foot high, and a foot from each other, set in a triangle, where the counties of Westmorland, Cumberland and Lancashire do meet together ...'.

The present Three Shire Stone had unusual beginnings. In 1816, a William Field was virtually the chief factotum in the small village of Cartmel, home of the lovely Priory. He was Bridge Master and thus responsible for the repair and maintenance of all bridges within the parish, as well as High Constable. He was also Stamp Distributor, (as once was Wordsworth, in Ambleside), Vestry Clerk at the Priory, (which would mean he recorded all the births, marriages and deaths in the parish) and Will-maker; a very busy and energetic man; a large fish in a small pool! An obvious enthusiast of his own county, Lancashire, (the sole county marked on the Three Shire Stone!) he ordered the cutting and carving of the Wrynose pillar; though why he did so and what his connection with Wrynose or the brandreth stones were, no one knows.

For nearly 45 years, until after William's death in 1860, the Three Shire Stone lay untouched in the entry opposite the Cavendish Arms Hotel, just off Cartmel village square. No one seemed interested in it until poor William died. Indeed, it is quite likely that at that time, very few villagers in Cartmel knew exactly where Wrynose was! Then, suddenly, as if realising William's past worth, and to make a lasting memorial to him, his relatives decided to carry out William's original project, and set up the limestone pillar on the top of the 'Stallion's Pass', Wrynose. Taken first by horse and cart from Cartmel to Hawkshead, it was then roped up to a team of horses, and dragged to the summit of the pass, where it was erected in its present position. No one seems to know what happened to the original brandreth

As the road over Wrynose descends into Little Langdale it passes the Pedder Stone (seen on the right) - a place where chapmen (pedlars) rested on the steep hill

stones, but they were drawn by an artist in 1852, and that small picture, by L.T.Aspland, is the sole pictorial record of these ancient boundary markers.

The descending road, twisting and turning steeply down the fellside into Little Langdale, passes a huge roadside boulder. This is the Pedder Stone, probably a corruption of Pedlar Stone, a place where exhausted chapmen, hard-working pedlars travelling on foot and too poor to own even a fell-pony to carry their load, rested their heavy pack on the table-like rock. Far below, at the base of the pass, are the chimneys of Fell Foot, with farm and buildings dating from the early 17th or possibly 16th century; indeed, some parts may be older still. The whitewashed house is old and attractive; but it is a veritable youngster compared to the table-topped mound behind it. This was the Viking dalesmen's *Thingmount*, or open-air parliament where only free men - those who owned their own land - were allowed access and free speech. First they had to leave all weapons stuck in the ground at the foot of the mound! Then, and only then, could they climb up and discuss their affairs with fellow-dalesmen on the flat, grassy top. It was a harsh but simple democracy - for the landowners. One wonders about any slaves owned, for pre-Christian Vikings had little concern for other humanity; capturing and selling men and women into slavery, keeping some, perhaps in abject serfdom. By the middle of the 10th century, however, many Cumbrian Vikings were Christian, and presumably, abhorred any form of slavery. Did this include most of the dalesmen of that time?

Fell Foot Farm and the Viking Thingmount, where parliaments were held

The farm, Fell Foot, was the store and depot of a notorious smuggler of the last century. He was Lanty Slee, Lanty being dialect for Lancelot, though this dalesman was far different to the Arthurian warrior of that name, the original 'gentil, parfait knight' of the Round Table legends. Lanty was the Cumbrian equivalent of the American 'moonshiner'. He distilled (illegally, of course!) a powerful brew made from potatoes; a crude but much sought-after whisky-liquor which he sold far and wide. Several of his stills were scattered over the fells; one in an old quarry and arranged so that the smoke from his still-fire was hidden and finally dispersed amongst the shattered rocks. Yet another still was high in the hills by Red Tarn above Wrynose, where the thirsty iron-ore miners scratching a living from the hard rock digging mountain haematite, were more than willing to co-operate with their "publican", their benefactor and visiting purveyor of powerful booze. The story is told and retold of Lanty's store at Fell Foot being raided by

Hackett Forge in Little Langdale. In the 17th century ore was brought down from Red Tarn and smelted here

customs officers though not before the occupants had been warned by that mysterious dales' 'telegraph' which functioned so well against any disliked authority. The frustrated officers could find no illicit booze; which was not surprising, for the farmer's wife, wearing the long black skirt usual in her time, held a huge skin-bladder of home-brew (hence the local expression of 'having a skinful' for being drunk) under her petticoats and stood, constantly and loudly berating the customs officers, who finally left, probably cursing the nagging old harridan!

By Fell Foot, the main road, if one dare call it that, heads east along the valley side. Another by-road leads off to the left, and climbs up and over into the sister and parallel valley of Great Langdale, passing the cold, Prussian-blue water of Blea Tarn on the way. It goes by an old house, huddled into the sloping fellside, part-sheltered by a windblasted ancient larch, with branches spreading like some raggy umbrella over the sturdy slate roof. This is the cottage written of by Wordsworth in the poem *The Excursion*, the home of his sad Solitary. In a harsh winter, it is a very lonely place, though the tourist traffic now passes by it in most seasons; it was, however, in old Westmorland, and therefore, need concern us no more.

A little way down the valley is yet another of those delightful fell cottages. Whitewashed, neat and attractive, it seems to have grown rather than have been built alongside the churning stream, here still beck-like rather than true river. This place, still known as Hackett Forge was once a busy iron works, despite its present remote and rural setting! It dates originally from 1603, though first mentioned as part of the iron-making industry in 1623. Then, the surrounding timber was *coled,* or made into charcoal as fuel for the forge and other nearby bloomeries, which were small and very crude iron-furnaces. After 1630, William Wright of Esthwaite (near Hawkshead), obtained a lease of:

> '... all that river or water within the manor of little Langdale commonlie called or knowne by the name of Haccat water or Langdale water and the banks and both sides thereof ... And also the dam and dik (dyke) thereunto belonging as the same are alreadie erected and made upp with libertie to pound (enclose) and stay the water issueing and coming to the forge or Iron works there standing and for making barre iron soe often as need shall require ...'.

The forge worked steadily on for very many more years. In 1653, it made a small profit (records are scanty) and by 1710 and 1711 had made over 30 tons of pig iron. By then, however, it was a refining furnace, processing bar iron made at Backbarrow on the River Leven. This was laboriously rowed or sailed up the length of Coniston Water by sturdy boatmen charging 1s 3d (6p) per load. The iron came from Backbarrow by packhorse to Nibthwaite, a hamlet on the south-eastern shore of the lake. Ferried up the lake it then came ashore finally at Waterhead, at the head of the lake, and thence, again by packhorse, made its way to Little Langdale, the cost of the road transport being one shilling - 5p in today's money - per bulky load! By 1726, iron-making methods were changing rapidly. Forty years later, by 1766, Hackett Forge had changed hands twice in a sharply competitive field, where such remote and increasingly antiquated works were being put out of commission. By 1818, a writer ignores any iron works and merely refers to the once-busy place as no more than 'a sheep stay amongst the mountains ...'. After that, Hackett Forge seems to have sunk into oblivion as an iron-making site.

The ore, mountain haematite, a blood-red rock with a very high percentage of natural iron, came from workings up in the hills due north of the top of Wrynose, close by Red Tarn. There, veins of the haematite are near the surface, providing rich ore and at the same time staining the greasy clay, a source of *reddle,* a natural red dye used to mark upland sheep. Reddle, mixed with thick grease to make it weatherproof, was used until quite recently. Each fell farm has a registered sheep-brand, a pop-mark peculiar to it, so that there was a constant demand for reddle. The lonely mines of Red Tarn even as early as the 17th century, supplied some 30 tons of ore in one year, every pound of it packhorsed down the mountainsides from these tiny mines set so high in a bowl of hills.

Not far beyond Fell Foot, long before reaching Hackett Forge, is the charming tarn of Little Langdale. Set in a bowl of hills, the water appears to change colour frequently, tinted by the moods of sky and scurrying cloud. It is a lovely place, fed by beck and mountain stream. One of these is marked by ancient, pollarded ash trees; the branches cut for tool handles long ago, the stout trunks now with a fuzz of thinner growth. In hard years, the ash leaves were fed to stock; not only do they keep well, but they are highly nutritious to sheep and cattle. In winter the tarn is a stopping-off place for the whooper swans, wild and regal birds from Iceland. The tarnside reeds, in summer, hold noisy sedge warblers and along the hurrying becks feeding the tarn, the yellow wagtail breeds. Yet, even in high summer, apart from the noise of stream water and the murmur of wind through the tarn-reeds, it may be a silent, lonely place; almost primeval, set amongst rocks still bearing the scratch and scar of ice travel of thousands of years ago. It may be sombre, according to weather; when dark, deep, silent water hurries away from the tarn, stirring a mass of bright yellow 'brandy bottles', yellow water lilies; flowers so-called from their odd-shaped seed containers, which writhe and sway on long, thin submerged stalks with every silent wimple and swirl of the strong current.

Nearby is Slaters' Bridge, a stone footbridge, where the arch seems likely to topple into the stream at any time, but one which has withstood the flood and fury for very many years. Just how long no one seems to know for some say it was built for the early 18th century quarrymen, enabling them to get to Hodge Close Quarry over the river. This may be true, but there was a

Slaters' Bridge, Little Langdale

Above: Newby Bridge

Right:
Walney Lighthouse

Above: Birks Bridge, Dunnerdale
Below: Coniston in winter (Photo: Walt Unsworth)

Slater family here 500 years ago in the 14th century, and the bridge certainly looks very old!

Little Langdale curves round, eventually, to join its sister dale of Great Langdale. Here, both broaden out, meeting at Elterwater, one of the true lakes of the Lake Counties, but narrower and shallower than most. This too is a shelter for overwintering whooper swans from Iceland, though perhaps with Martin Mere, near Southport and Slimbridge in the West Country playing host to so many winter wildfowl, (and making sure they remain well fed throughout the winter), the Elterwater whoopers do not tarry here for long. They pass through very quickly, the lake now being little more than resting place and temporary stay for them after the flight from Iceland. Elterwater has held varying numbers of whooper swans every winter for a very long time; the name of the lake proves it, for modern "Elterwater" is a corrupted form of the old Norse *Elptrvatn*, which means, quite simply the 'Lake of the Wild Swans'!

Downstream from the dark lake, the former Little Langdale stream, now the fast-running, wider River Brathay, bounds over a steel-hard lip of rock, in the crash and thunder of Skelwith Force, a magnificent waterfall. Though little more than 12 or 15 feet high, it is a mighty torrent for much of the year, impressive enough even in the rare times of drought, when the river is very low. Tourists visit it by the hundred, but it remains a lovely place. Go there early in the morning, soon after sun up and see the white water turn to gold and the fine spray produce one glorious rainbow after another. Or in winter wander by the woods at the edge of the lake, where one might see those quaint and ugly birds, crossbills, with twisted, scissor-like beaks for tearing out the seeds of pine cones. There is the chance of watching a magnificent drake goosander on the still lake water, or diving goldeneye, or white-flanked tufted drakes. Herons fish here frequently and more rarely, the dowdy, furtive cormorants dive after yellow-bellied eels in the dark lake water. The bushes, some with feet in the lake, are interesting. One species here is a balsam popular the 'Balm of Gilead'. How it came here is unknown, for it is an introduction from Canada or the U.S.A. It has a wonderful resinous scent when the buds open, particularly after rain. Once smelt, it can never be forgotten.

The Brathay, now a full and splendid force, ripples on towards the distant lake, now near the road, now away from it, until it finally pours into Windermere with its shorter, and formerly Westmerian twin, the bounding Rothay. There, where it flows by Borrans Field, the site of the old Roman fort of Galava, at the head of *Vinund's mere*, it enters old Westmorland and is beyond the scope of this book.

8: Two Lakeland Towns

WAY BACK in the mid-12th century, when old Norse was probably still the normal everyday language of the area, the village of Coniston was enscribed as *Coningeston.* The first part of the word is very close to a phonetic rendering of the old Danish word *Kunung* and in this first record would be written down, most likely, by a clerk in holy orders more used to speaking and writing in Norman-French or mediaeval Latin rather than in any form of the old Viking tongue. In fact, the name Conisgeton, and the Konisgeton of 40 years later, are ancient hybrids; each is a direct mix from two words; one the original Danish-Scandinavian *Kunung*, meaning king, and the other, *tun, a* word in old English (a language sometimes called Anglo-Saxon), and generally, meaning anything from a hamlet or manor to a single small farm.

"So what?" says the reader. Well, it does matter quite a lot to anyone with the slightest interest in history. Broken down, the old form of the name means that Coniston was once a royal farm of some kind, a settlement, or perhaps part of a manor, which belonged to some long dead and now unknown Saxon king. He was not the ruler of the English nation, or even a tribe, but much more likely, a petty tyrant or monarch, an overlord of a comparatively small area around Coniston over which he had assumed power. Again, from the place-name type, it can be shown that the original old English Coniston was eventually taken over by Norsemen, and that some of these local Vikings were Danish, rather than from western Norway, or Norse-Irish like many of the Scandinavians occupying so much of western Cumbria about a thousand years ago. This in turn, may give one an insight into any land-practices in use over the centuries and provide important clues to the long social and economic history of the immediate region.

For one thing the Saxons, great corn-eaters, were arable farmers growing oats, barley and wheat as staples. The cereal grown in any one area was according to the soil-type, altitude, aspect and local climate; accordingly, these ancient English were experts at seeking out ideal growing soil. The early English also used water-powered mills to grind these cereals into various kinds of flour or meal. The Norseman, on the other hand, immigrant Icelander, Norse-Irishman, Western Norwegian, Finn, Swede, or Dane (and all these ancient settlers are represented in Cumbria), was primarily a sheep farmer. So, merely by one place-name, we have a glimpse of two distinctly

The Walna Scar road, an ancient trackway over the Coniston Fells. Photo : Walt Unsworth

different peoples, as well as their widely differing ways of life.

Yet even this land tenure of a thousand and more years ago is comparatively new; it pales rapidly into insignificance when compared with the inhabitants of Coniston who came there long before Saxon or Scandinavian. The first traces of human settlement in the area belong to Bronze Age people of perhaps four millennia and more ago. Their crude stone circles and turf-and-stone-walled cattle compounds and village-enclosures were sited high up on the flatter part of Banniside Moor, high above the present town of Coniston, on a shoulder of the fell immediately south of the mountains which tower above the town. These people were sheep farmers, too, for a fragment of woollen cloth, the only one of its type in Britain, was found in a burial tumulus here. Given to Coniston museum, it went missing some time in the 1920s, and has never been found again. Which is very sad; for with today's technology the woven cloth may well have shown the breed of sheep herded by these ancient and gifted people. These mysterious folk, which the late W.G.Collingwood, one-time Professor of Viking Life and Literature in Cambridge University, called, with good cause because of their upland situation, 'The Children of the Mist'.

The Coniston cloth fragment might have proved a prehistoric origin for the Herdwick breed of sheep, native only to the Lake District. Or, as the police sometimes say, by close examination of the woollen fibres of the Bannisdale cloth, eliminated the tough little Herdwick 'from our enquiries'.

By all accounts, the woven cloth fragment was bi-coloured, from natural wool-colour rather than plant-dye. Which could suggest the use of the dark, cocoa-brown wool of the young Herdwick, a first-winter animal, woven in a pattern with the grey wool of a Herdwick more than a year old. I suspect that the Coniston cloth was rather like the Romano/British checks and neutral coloured weave of similar cloth found during modern excavations of Vindolanda, a Roman fort and civil settlement close by Hadrian's Wall. Some of these specimens, however, have been dyed, using rose-madder, lichens, and other plant substances.

The area in which these Bronze Age herdsmen above Coniston lived lies on the broad southern shoulder of the Coniston massif. An ancient track, Walna Scar, crosses the upland, passing from Coniston and over into Dunnderdale, the valley of the River Duddon, linking up with routes to the west coast. The present pathway, gouged deep by a combination of tourist boots and erosion by freeze-thaw and rainwash, was once beautifully paved. It may have been mediaeval work, a narrow highway constructed, maintained and repaired under Furness Abbey authority. This institution was the greatest of Furness landowners during the Middle Ages and the structure and maintenance of such an important highway would enable trade, easy travel, and quick communication between the many areas of Abbey interest. Some, hopefully, think the track Roman, but so far, sadly, with no evidence of any Roman track or occupation in the rest of Furness, except across its northern boundary in the elbow of Dunnerdale leading up to Wrynose Pass, this seems to be wishful thinking.

There is no guesswork involved in the presence of the stone circles up on the open moorland of Banniside, however. These prehistoric rings of stone are small, and probably sepulchral, meaning they are burial markers rather than lunar or solar calendars. Close by them, near Walna Scar, is a Bronze Age compound, marked on two sides by a turf and cobble wall base, which was probably originally topped by briar, thorn, or sharpened wooden stakes, to keep out wolves, bears, lynx, or other cattle and sheep-predators active in that district in that prehistoric time.

The *Scar* of Walna Scar means a ridge, in this case one going up and over into the next valley; a travellers route from time out of mind. I believe it to be a track down which hunter-gatherers, stone-axe and bronze traders all passed in turn; a route known to early Celt, Saxon, Dane, and Norwegian; travellers and traders ranging over thousands of years; even, possibly, a road used by patrolling Romans, ever alert to the dangers of ambush and attack by hostile people in an equally savage environment. Perhaps those using this track more than anyone, except the many walkers and climbers

Coniston and the Coppermines Valley. Photo: Walt Unsworth

of today, were the hard-working copper miners of the 18th and 19th centuries.

The Coniston massif is the range of mountains looking down onto the present small town. In these mountains, the hard rock bears rich veins of copper and in much lesser quantity, other metalliferous ores. Most were originally hydrothermal deposits according to the geologists, in which a boiling hot solution or gas was forced up and through the native rock by heat below the earth's crust millions of years ago. The gases cooled and condensed, the liquid settling pipe-like in the hard rock, the minerals coming out of solution to form mineral veins of various length and size, many of them the rich ore-lodes exploited by the miners. Mining in the Coniston hills went on for many years with increasing efficiency, until, by last century, the shafts eventually became too deep to pump clear the water constantly pouring into the workings from the surface. This flooding and the rocketing expense of continuous pumping, soon made the extraction of ore more and more difficult and expensive. At the same time, imported foreign ore became increasingly cheaper as more high grade copper deposits which could be worked by open cast or shallow surface mining were discovered abroad. Finally, the water-pumping load, plus the importation of cheap foreign ore was too much; the Coniston copper mines finally ceased working. Today, their adits or mine drains, together with other tunnels, old shafts, and a variety of industrial remains and remnants are scattered in many areas about Coniston. One of these is the great upland bowl of Red Dell, a place better known today as Coppermines Valley. It is not just a junk heap, a graveyard of wrecked industry; but a fascinating site of industrial archaeology, with white-breasted dippers in the swift streams, and parson-collared ring-ousels chattering amongst the tumbled stone every high summer. All of it is barely a mile from the *Black Bull* pub, in Coniston's main street, and soon reached by a path behind it.

This track rises rapidly towards the old mine workings and the Coniston Youth Hostel, passing along and across the bounding falls and rapids of Church Beck. As clear as crystal, the water still has the aquamarine shade of copper sulphate solution in the deeper pools, though I am assured that this has nothing to do with any dissolved minerals within it. This water, we have been told by an analytical chemist dealing with such things, is amongst the purest in the world, and does not contain any copper at all! Indeed, it contains nothing but the barest trace of any mineral. Red Dell, once the site of the major mine workings, echoes with the sound of running water. It is a huge and fascinating memorial to an industrial age, but it is a place slowly reverting to nature; it may be also dangerous to the stupid or the foolhardy, who insist on entering the old workings, some of which have deep shafts going straight down to deeper levels, hundreds of feet below. Incidentally, I do not include the very professional and careful cavers and the like in that list; they also venture within these mines, but do so with care and skill. These old mines may hold unwitting and deadly death-traps. One particular trap for the unwary is the long disused shaft, a vertical descent to lower levels perhaps hundreds of feet deep, cut into a mine-passage floor! This was a common practice.

Though there are hints and suggestions, but with no certain facts to back them, that Romans may have worked the copper here, the Coniston complex was first worked by professional miners in 1599. At this time, a group of Germans, employed by an Augsberg company, began work at Coniston. Previously, they had worked the mines about Keswick under licence from Queen Elizabeth I. One such German, called Simon, is remembered by Simon's Nick, a pronounced slot in the skyline. This was part of a huge copper vein, the rich metal extracted and followed downhill; but it is also the place mentioned in the local folk-tale. Here, poor Simon, allegedly in league with the Devil (as long as he could be assured of plentiful copper ore) was destroyed by the evil one struggling for his soul. If truth be known, it would seem that 'in league with the devil' was a local interpretation of gunpowder knowledge and the engineering practice of mining, something not possessed by many locals at that time. Quite likely, too, Simon was blown up by the self-same stuff, when using a fuse which was either faulty, or too short. Some fuses, for example, were nothing more than long straws, carefully filled with black powder. They were erratic, to say the least and more than one cottage was blasted when miners prepared these fuses at home, by the hearth, the room lit by candle light!

The many traces of copper mining under the mountains to be seen here today are usually of 19th century working. The spoil heaps sometimes yield small fragments of the copper ore sought by the miners; copper pyrites, which gleams like gold. Or malachite, a wonderful blue green, not unlike some tints of modern eyeshadow. The soldiers of Cleopatra as well as the lady herself used malachite. For Cleopatra it was a cosmetic, for the soldiers, rubbed around their eyes, it was a protectant against the glare of sun on the desert sand! Eskimos used soot from simple whale-oil or blubber lamps in similar fashion to protect eyes from the constant white glare of snow.

The other important copper ore, azurite, which as its name implies is a breathtaking sky-blue, is also present, and both are eagerly sought by collectors. Pieces of either mineral, green or blue, are now hard to find. Coniston, as a town owes its presence to three things; obviously and firstly there were the rich and extensive copper mines, worked for more than three centuries. The second reason is the huge slate quarries, mostly abandoned. The strangely named Bursting Stone quarry in the southern face of the mountain called Coniston Old Man is still being worked and is now a source of controversy between those demanding the retention of all natural beauty, and those eager to keep native trades going and utilise the magnificent rock. Coniston slate is a lovely shade of green, pallid and unmistakable, still much in demand at many places all over the world.

The third industry, thriving more than ever these days, is tourism, which really got into its stride in the early days of Queen Victoria and has increased in importance ever since. Being at the head of a lake which afforded easy transport of heavy goods up or down it by boat was a point in early Coniston's favour, particularly before the development of good roads. Copper, ore, slate, and gunpowder from the works beside that other lovely lake, Elterwater, were all shipped down Coniston Water to the creek ports of Greenodd and Ulverston in the late 18th and early 19th centuries as already mentioned.

A railway line (first started as one to haul away the slate and copper in

Tourists now sail Coniston Water on the restored "Gondola". Photo: Walt Unsworth

Victorian times) was here until 1966, until removed on the advice of the ruthless Dr Beeching. The line ran down to the Duddon estuary and joined the main west coast line by the sea at Foxfield. This Foxfield/Coniston line could have been a marvellous tourist attraction; a wonderful way of entering the Lake District from the west, passing from seashore to the feet of the mountains through delightful countryside; but it has gone forever. The track was pulled up years ago, the route grassed over, or fenced in and rapidly changed to private land or garden.

The line has vanished and so, very much earlier, did the passenger steamer on Coniston Water, which sailed from the foot of the lake to the head. In its place now-a-days is, of course, the delightful, rebuilt *Gondola,* a small and beautiful vessel. She is in limited service but can accommodate people with elegance and great comfort.

Coniston Water is more than five miles in length. Somewhere beneath the usually placid surface lie the bones of Donald Campbell, killed in his attempt on the world's water speed record in 1967. His famous *Bluebird* somersaulted when travelling at maximum speed and blew up, taking Donald with her to the bottom of the lake. His body has never been found but he is remembered by a delightful, if simple, memorial by the car park in the town.

The lake was known, amongst other things as *Turstini wattra*, a form of 'Thorstein's water' in a crude mediaeval mixture of language and dialect. Thorstein's Mere is another very old name for the lake; one in use for centuries before being changed into the present and rather prim Coniston Water. Who this unknown Viking who gave his name to the lake was, no one knows. The lake island is Peel, a name which has certain connotations with a fort, or stout refuge, like the 14th century pele towers; the small stone keeps built throughout Cumbria as hasty refuge against Scots raiders.

The same Peel Island on Coniston Water was the site of much material for Arthur Ransome's delightful and nostalgic *Swallows and Amazons* series of childrens' books. It was never a true pele, but possibly one man's refuge against invaders or an oppressive mediaeval society. It is much more likely that it was the home of a hermit. Perhaps the retreat of a local wise man; but not one without cupidity and a keen business sense, who, in a time when the church was all-powerful and demand for religious artifacts great, made and sold religious lead badges and tiny brooches. A mould for this has been found on the island! There are traces of other and more industrialised metal-makers scattered about the lake shore, usually near a stream. These relics of past industry are the cinders and the slag of old bloomeries; the mark of iron-makers of the years before, during, and after the time of Elizabeth I. Amongst the shoreside trees, there are also overgrown pitsteads, circular platforms, where from unrecorded historical times right up to the 1920s, men made charcoal in the leafy summer woods.

There is much to see and discover in and about Coniston; the museum there is excellent and gives many clues. So does Coniston Hall, former home of the le Fleming family, a branch of those first landing at Aldingham on the northern shore of Morecambe Bay in the early 12th century. The present Hall, though built on an ancient site, is largely 17th century with some parts of the fabric much older. It has huge rooms, thick stone walls, and massive, rounded, Westmorland type chimneys. Amongst many other historical involvements, it was a Captain Fleming, a member of the family then living at Coniston Hall, who reported the advance of the Armada up the English Channel to Francis Drake!

Hawkshead, five miles to the east of Coniston, is also set at the head of a lake, Esthwaite Water, which is much shallower and smaller than that of Coniston. There is no confusion about the origin of this place name! It is pure old Norse, slightly corrupted by clumsy modern tongues. Hawkshead is really *Haakon's saetr* the summer pasture of Haakon who with a name like

The mediaeval courthouse at Hawkshead

that most certainly was Norse, or of Viking background!

Hawkshead was a market town, and here the two principal trades were in wool and slate quarrying. The woollen goods included knitting wool as well as thousands of pairs of stockings knitted annually from locally spun Herdwick wool - always in demand, particularly amongst the hardworking dalesfolk throughout the district. The shallow lake provided plenty of fish which were sold at the market, though this was never very important to the town's economy. Three miles away to the east is the Windermere ferry, so that direct shipment of goods across the lake to Windermere and the busier market and trading centre of Kendal was comparatively easy.

Today, Hawkshead depends almost entirely on tourists for its income. There are a few farms, but the once busy corn mill has long gone and the bustling weekly market of a century and more ago is vanished. The once elitist 16th century Grammar School, which amongst other pupils, held Wordsworth, is no longer a school. The mediaeval Court House built by the monks of Furness Abbey, who made Hawkshead an important wool-gathering centre and rich Abbey grange, is now reduced to a museum; which is quite a come-down for a place where once the Abbot's minions were almost regal in their authority. They had power of life or death over any residents coming before them in this striking old courthouse at the north end of the village.

Hawkshead is a lovely place, despite the frequent crowds of tourists. Look at the old walls and windows, the massive rounded Westmorland and other chimneys, the narrow ginnels (the passages between houses and other buildings). It will be seen that the houses huddle about a centre, which some say was for mutual protection against any hostile attack. More sensible is the suggestion that the houses protected winter cattle, which could be driven in here for shelter during the severest weather. Explore the village slowly; take it all in, and then go and look at the old grammar school. Finally, within the town, go to the church, standing on its own green hill and overlooking the long expanse of Esthwaite water.

The church, once but no more a chapel of ease under Dalton, far to the southwest, was formerly whitewashed. This was changed to roughcast years ago, which spoilt the effect. The present building, on a hill like so many of its kind, has both Norman and Georgian parts within the fabric, but it is on a very ancient site. Within it are two effigies of the Sandys, man and wife of the early 16th century, in dress of that time, and she with a pug-nosed dog at her feet. One member of this distinguished family became Archbishop of York; but that was a long time ago. The land by the church was the gathering ground for those unfortunates involved in the Pilgrimage of Grace, an appeal, amongst other things, to Henry VIII to restore the old Catholic religion.

During World War II the churchyard held an unusual occupant; Bernard Brandt, first officer of a German U-boat, the *U570*. His story is bizarre, for his ship was captured and later put into service by the Royal Navy as *HMS Graph*. Brandt had surrendered *U570* to a Coastal Command aircraft, a Lockheed Hudson and when he was brought as a prisoner to the high security camp at nearby Grisedale Hall, (pulled down long ago) Brandt was tried by fellow senior German Officers in a secret kangaroo court held within the camp unknown to the British guards. This 'Court of Honour' as it dubbed itself, was presided over by Germany's premier U-boat ace, Otto Kretschmer, a prisoner of war captured a few weeks earlier than Brandt when attacking an Atlantic convoy.

Condemned to death by the court Brandt promised instead to escape and sabotage his own vessel, then lying in Barrow docks being refitted by Vickers naval dockyard. He managed to escape, but was found wandering in Grisedale forest shortly afterwards by a suspicious Home Guard patrol. Asked to explain his presence he panicked and made a run for it. One Home Guard shouted to him to stop but as Brandt continued to run away, aimed a shot at his legs. As luck would have it, poor Brandt stumbled at that instant and the bullet, meant for his legs, hit him in the back and killed him

This young oak marks the spot where Thomas Lancaster was hung in chains 'until his bones fell to pieces', for poisoning his family

instantly. He was granted a full military funeral - despite it being wartime, the time of the desperate Battle of the Atlantic, and with high feeling running against any U-boat crew. Brandt's body was eventually taken back to Germany after the war, and reburied near his home town.

Beyond Hawkshead church, on the road to Windermere ferry, and not far beyond the car park, the road crosses a beck. The road formerly ran across a marsh and this kind of road usually built on a bank clear of the wet marsh peat, was known as a *causeway*, soon shortened to *causey* in local dialect. The bridge over the central stream has a fence on each side made up of Victorian iron panels, painted a vivid green. On the right, immediately over the beck, there is a young oak tree growing in what was once a sodden marsh. This tree marks the gallows where Thomas Lancaster, 17th century poisoner, was hung in chains.

The following extract from the oldest parish Register Book of Hawkshead church tells it all:

> '1672, April 8. Thomas Lancaster who for poysonninge his owne family was Adjudg't att the Assizes att Lancaster to bee carried backe to his owne house att Hyewrey where hee lived: and was there hang'd before his owne doore till hee was dead, for that very facte then was brought with a horse and carr into the Coulthouse meadows and forthwith hunge upp in iron Chaynes on a Gibbet which was sett for that very purpose on the south=syde of Sawrey Casey neare unto the Pool-stang: and there continued untill such tymes as hee rotted everye bone from other...'

Thomas Lancaster was brought before Sir Daniel Fleming, of Rydal Hall. He wrote:

The Quaker-meeting house of Colthouse near Hawkeshead built in 1688

'Being lately in Lancashire, I received there...information against one Thomas Lancaster, late of Threlkeld in Cumberland, who, it is very probable, hath committed the most horrid act that hath been heard of in this countrey. He marryed 30th January last a wife in Lancashire, who was agreed to be marryed that very day or soon after, to another; and her father afterwards conveyed all his reall estate to this Lancaster upon giveing him security to pay severall sums of money to himself and his daughters. And through covetousness to save these and other payments, Lancaster hath lately poysoned - with white arsenic - his wife, her father, her three sisters, her aunt, her cosingerman (cousin), and a servant boy, besides poyson given to severall of his neighbours - who are and have been sick - that people - as it is presumed might think the rest dyed of a violent fever.....I have committed his prisoner to Lancaster Castle, and shall take what more evidence I can meet with or discover.....'.

In the 17th century Hawkshead became a centre for the Nonconformists. The Quakers were one such body and by the mid-17th century they had their own burial ground. This was at Colthouse, at the end of Sawrey causey, where a short track leads away from the Windermere ferry road. The first burial made in the Colthouse graveyard is recorded thus: 'Burials 1658. ffeb. Xth: Agnes, the wife of Edward rigge de Hye Wray, Quaker which was buryed at Culthouse in George Braithwt packe (paddock) the same beinge an Intended buryinge place for that sect, and shee the first

Corps which was layde therein...'. This makes the burial ground one of the first ever made solely for Quakers. George Fox, the Quaker movement's founder, did not enter Furness before 1652 and the Colthouse paddock was bought only 6 years later. The Colthouse Meeting House was not built until 1688, however, and during that time the Quakers would meet at one and anothers' houses, which made them prime targets for those in authority. The Colthouse farms and houses of these gentle people are still intact, their Meeting House is still in use and their graveyard still a peaceful, gentle place. It is a small, grassy meadow, fitted with wall seats of thick slate slabs, the ground white with snowdrops each and every February.

The early Quakers allowed no gravestones, feeling them 'a worldley vanytie', but here, some of the first types of headstone allowed (from the late 18th or early 19th century), stand in neat rows. Most are small, with rounded top, the later type often of purple Welsh slate. Many bear nothing but the name of the grave occupant and sometimes, the date of death.

Past records of the persecution of the Quakers and other Dissenters in Cumbria make chilling reading. The blatant (and legal) persecution, theft, and extortion of the 17th century Cumbrian Quakers is something terrible to realise. They were robbed of goods and livestock, (often the best of both), made to pay extortionate fines, threatened with transportation to the colonies and even death; all in the name of the Christian religion!

The persecution stemmed from the passing of the Conventicle Act of 1664, which stated that '.....every person above sixteen attending any Dissenting meeting (a Protestant meeting other than that of the established Church of England) was liable to imprisonment for three months, or a fine of £5 for the first offence, double for the second, and a fine of £100, or seven years transportation to the American plantations, from which escape was death ...'.

One court record of the Colthouse Quakers says it all: '16th January, 1684: George Braithwaite for suffering the conventicle above (a meeting at his house): the sum of £20.0.0...'. This was a huge sum for a farmer of those days, but even poor William Atkinson, a humble tanner, also present at the conventicle was fined ten shillings, together with several more people. The wives present were also fined five shillings each, and because one unknown man at the meeting escaped without being identified, four of the others then had to give £5 each to make up the unknown person's fine of £20!

It should be remembered that this time was not long after the Civil War, which had been won by the forces of Cromwell. With the restoration of the monarchy in 1662, when Charles II was restored to the throne, the Royalist party came back into favour: thus in many areas, there were old scores to settle between the now-triumphant Royalists and those formerly 'of the Parliamentary Party', which continued to be so well-favoured by the majority of the Dissenters. Thus, all Dissenters, particularly the Quakers, were the prime target for any Royalist authority.

It is sad to talk of so many old, unhappy, far-off things. Instead, consider Esthwaite Water; it is rich in natural history with wildfowl ranging from Canada geese to sawbilled mergansers crowding the lake in winter; birds like tiny dabchick and elegant, ruffed Great crested grebes breed here in summer. It is a lake of surprises such as that of several years ago, when the nutrias arrived here. Nutrias? Most people know them as coypu, the giant 'water-rats', which they are not. They are South American rodents, rather beaver-like aquatic mammals, first introduced to this country in fur-farming. Escaping from the fur farms, they became established in the former Fen Country of East Anglia for decades. In eastern England they were pests of the sugar beet fields for years, but how did they reach Esthwaite Water, miles away, and up in Cumbria? The Esthwaite coypu are no more and by now, after a rigorous extermination campaign, none are left in East Anglia.

The old pack-horse route to Kendal from Hawkshead followed the line of the present road through Sawrey and so on down to the ferry. Because the first stretch of track on the Hawkshead side was over boggy ground, the causeway already mentioned was built. It is interesting to know that the present causey was not the first; traces of one which used a base of juniper branches and ling, over which gravel was tipped, were found last century, and for a time, there was speculation that this may have been Roman.

The late date of the introduction of wheeled vehicles in the district is remarkable. The so-called roads were little better than tracks and transport of goods was always by individual horse or by one of the regular pack-horse trains. Travellers went on foot or on horseback until 1792 when, for the first time, a 'chaise driver' is mentioned in local records. As late as 1819, a guidebook reported that '...there are several decent inns at Hawkshead, but only one post-chaise, kept at the *Red Lion*'.

Nor did winter weather, or seasonal storms help the very bad state of the roads. There is a remarkable 17th century record of a summer storm which caused great havoc in the district:

> 'Bee it remembered that upon the tenth day of June att nighte in the yeare of our lord the one thousand sixxe hundred eighty and sixxe there was such a fearefull Thunder with fyre and rayne which occasioned such a terrible flood as the like of it was never seene in these parts by noe man liveinge; for it did throwe downe some houses and

> milles and tooke Away severall briggs (bridges); yea the water did run through houses and did much hurte to houses; besydes the water wash't upp greate trees by roots and the becks and gills carried them with other greate trees stocks and greate stones a greate way off and layd them on men's ground; yea further the water did soe freely run down the hye-ways and made such deep holes and ditches in them that att severall places neither horse nor foote coulde passe; and besydes the becks and rivers did so breake out of their races as they broughte exceeding great sand beds into men's ground att many places which did greate hurte the never like was knowne...'.

Those who dare to complain of Cumbrian weather, or the cynics who say a path and a beck in Lakeland are synonymous' please note - and take heed!

More than fifty years ealier a similar storm sank the ferry crossing Windermere from the Lancashire side when 'Upon the 19th day of October 1630 the Great Boat upon Windermere water sunck about sun setting, when was drowned fforty seaven persons and eleaven horses: ffrom suden Death Libera nos..'. The disaster also created a mystery, for though the victims are all carefully listed by name, the nature of their travel is still a cause for argument. Traditionally, they were all members of a wedding party, crossing the lake after the wedding of Thomas Benson, a yeoman farmer from Bowness and Elizabeth Sawrey, both of whom were supposedly buried beneath the yew trees in Bowness churchyard. Yet neither of their names appear in the list of victims, though again an entry in the Kendal records of that time reads '...19th October Thomas Miller, boatman and 47

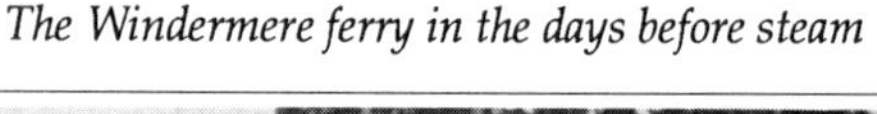

The Windermere ferry in the days before steam

The old steam powered ferry with a coachload of passengers

men and women were drowned in Windermere water, with 9 or 10 horses, having been at a wedding...'. Yet the wedding quoted above took place on the 15th of the month, four days earlier than the ferry tragedy. Moreover, the 19th was Hawkshead Market Day, so it is likely that the victims were returning from market rather than attending a wedding. Poor 'Thomas Milner, boatman' as he is called in the published list, also lost his two daughters travelling with him. I wonder who the poor little 'servant maide of Kendall' was? She was one of the few victims not fully named in the list.

The Windermere ferry was an old institution before the accident; the small estate there, later furnished with an inn, was called Boat. It is the obvious place for a ferry, for here, between two projecting nabs of rock, the lake is at its narrowest, being no more than 500 yards wide. For many years, it was in the hands of the Braithwaite family.

A ruined building just off the road down to the crossing was a station; a fashionable 18th century place from which to view the scenery. Providing refreshments and simple services for the quality, it fell into disuse when fashions changed and these approved stations were disregarded by an increasing number of humbler tourists.

Boat, or sometimes *Great Boat*, which became the *Ferry Hotel*, at the edge of Windermere on the former Lancashire side, was the scene of many wrestling events in earlier times. These may well have started with the

The Ferry Hotel was the scene of wrestling and other sports, later transferred to Grasmere

Great Frost of 1785, when 'a great wrestling, with a Kendal band of music, and plenty of good cheer was held on the ice...'. The lake was frozen solid, with people crossing with ease from one side of the lake to the other, crowds skating, some of the bolder spirits on horseback and others with horse and light cart, plus young bloods dashing about with horse and chaise. To entertain the crowds, one of the chief attractions was Cumberland and Westmorland style wrestling, exactly as practised at Grasmere and other Lakeland sports today except that on the ice, those 18th century performers wore clogs!

Miles and James Dixon were typical; they were dry-stone wallers from Hawkshead and very hardy men. Both were 6 feet 3 inches tall, Miles weighing in at fifteen and a half stones, his brother a mere fourteen! The lighter man was overall champion of the Ferry meets in 1811, his brother not far behind. A third brother, George, was smaller and bandy-legged, but still strong enough to throw Rowan Long. Rowan was a woodcutter by trade, an enormous man with more strength than skill. On steep slopes in the woods, where no horse could stand, he would put himself in the shafts and haul the timber down to flatter ground: nothing for a lad who weighed 17 stone and stood 6 feet 2 inches tall at 17, and who fought later at 18 stone! Between 1796 and 1812 he won no less than 99 belts but strive as he could, he never won a final one to complete the 100! He retired in 1824, and became a market gardener. When Rowan died in 1852 the coffin holding him measuring 27 inches across the breast on the inside! John Long, another and smaller wrestler, was sheep-shearer, woodcutter and later on, chief boatman at the Ferry. He died at the inn on Kirkstone Pass in 1848. Of them all, perhaps William Wilson was the most remarkable. He was six foot four, and weighted 15 stones; he is best remembered for hip-throwing and defeating John McLaughlan, an enormous Highlander, who was 6 feet 6 inches tall and weighed more than 20 stones! Another wrestler of renown of rather more recent times was Thomas Longmire, who died in 1899. Known to the great Charles Dickens, he was once the proprietor of the *Hole in the Wall* Inn, Bowness, and is remembered today by a plaque fixed to its outside wall. Tom won many cups and belts. He retired in 1860, but became a popular umpire at such events. In 1880, Tom was presented with a silver salver for his services to the sport. *The Ferry Hotel* wrestling bouts became an annual event, but in 1861, the venue was changed to Grasmere, and the great Lakeland sports tradition was born!

These wrestlers of yesteryear were quite literally giants among men; but who, crossing the quiet and delightful ferry today, would ever think the hotel grounds had played host to these huge athletes and the shouting, exciting crowds which followed their every move?

The 'Hole-in-the-Wall,' Bowness, visited by Charles Dickens when champion wrestler Thomas Longmire was host

9: The Woodlands

MANY CENTURIES AGO, Lancashire north of the Sands was well endowed with forest. In Roman times, the Lakeland hills and mountains were clothed with trees, in some places up to the present 2000-foot contour line. Though this is far from true today, there are yet some interesting stretches of woodland, and at least one official Forest, that of Grizedale, within the area described. My favourite stretch of woodland is that of Appletreeworth, which is rather off the usual tracks taken by most tourists. To get there, one way is to leave the square at Broughton-in-Furness, and take the road running almost due north (straight ahead out of the square) which is signposted to Broughton Mills and Coniston.

This road branches off to the left about two miles further on, the right bend taking one towards Torver and Coniston, the smaller side road leading to Broughton Mills, a hamlet tucked down in the bottom of the valley. Before descending the steep hill down to the River Lickle and the Mills hamlet, a road branches off to the right and curving, climbs along the ridge between two obvious valleys. That on the left belongs to the Lickle; the right hand side being a broader valley carved out over the ages by the fast running Torver Beck. This road along the windswept ridge between the two valleys goes by an old barn, which has a curious block of red sandstone set in the southern wall, bearing initials N.E. on top, the letter P in the centre, and the initials S.M. below it. The date 1742 is at the base of the stone. A similarly shaped slab, also of red sandstone and shaped rather like a gravestone, is in the front wall of Carter Ground, a fell farm over to the north-west, which suggests the same architect, or the same owner. Both Carter Ground farm and this roadside building are high above the Lickle valley.

This old barn by the road has the grandiose and appropriate title of Height House. It was once an inn, a welcome resting place for packhorsemen, weary chapmen, and cattle-drovers coming from West Cumberland by way of the Duddon fords, or later, by the bridge over the river and making their way across country to Ulverston, Kendal, or Lancaster markets. Both old road and one-time pub are gone; the former road reduced to a little-used, little known grassy track winding over the fields and fells; the lonely pub now nothing more than a barn with half the roof gone. It is an eerie place when the strong sou'westerlies growl in the tattered slates and the wind roars through the hedges.

Further along the ridge, beyond the battered old barn, the road, as with most of those over fell-land or peat moss, rises and dips continually, before plunging sharply downhill to meet yet another stream and an old bridge. The steam is a tributary of the tiny Lickle; the bridge is Howk Bridge, an ancient arch of grey stone spoilt by the modern addition of iron hand-rails. The beck in its narrow, boulder-littered bed, is well screened by hazel, alder, willow and oak trees. The water with its lines of trees is a border to a huge area of forestry woodland known as Appletreeworth. The southern gate into it is by an ample area of grass for parking. Beyond the gate, on foot, you may wander where you will and with common sense, go where you please. It is a delightful area, a plantation of almost a thousand acres. Such a lovely place for walks and picnics, with wide tracks, grassy fire-breaks between the rows of trees, crags well draped with heather and ling, and the mouldering walls of a tiny settlement (which could be of Bronze age date) tucked into a tiny upland hollow.

The name Appletreeworth is a puzzle; it is old English, amongst upland

Appletreeworth, now belonging to the Forestry Commission

which is almost otherwise entirely labelled in old Norse! *Apple* in the old Saxon tongue may mean any kind of fruit borne on tree or bush and not necessarily the cultivated kind of an orchard. Why should the title of the place be Saxon in origin? Again no one knows. Perhaps it was the farm of a Saxon specialising in fruit and not, like so many of his contemporaries, ordinary arable farming? And why, with such an unusual name (and product, if the name be true) dating back to Saxon times are there no old records of the place? It would seem to have been a unique farm at one time, but the lack of evidence for its early existence is mystifying.

This adds to the interest of the whole place. Speculation of origin may run riot, but what is really there is a huge area of woodland belonging to the Forestry Commission, much of it planted with conifers. Cedar, spruce, fir, pine (including Lodge pole pine, the tree species used by the Red Indians for their tepee poles!), and larch are well represented in great variery. One deciduous tree worth noting is the Red Oak, with huge leaves of bright scarlet every autumn. It is a North American species, always very lovely at the backend of the year. The Western red cedars, which smell delightfully of fresh pineapple, border the stream on the right. On the left, the steep face of a bluff line holds the dark mouth of an ancient lead mine. Alongside this is a peculiar geological feature called slickensides, where one rock surface has slipped over another, and wherein the two surfaces develop polished, smooth stone marked with linear grooves and ridges parallel to the direction of former movement.

The shaley stones about the foot of the mine and the shattered rock used as surface cover on the forestry tracks reveal some fascinating and unusual fossils. These are only seen if one looks very carefully at the shattered rock.

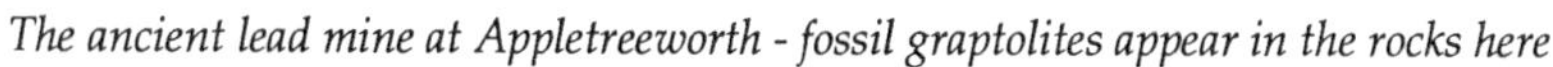

The ancient lead mine at Appletreeworth - fossil graptolites appear in the rocks here

They appear as strange and beautiful patterns, black against the darker rock and difficult to see. Many are *graptolites*, tiny, colonial animals of ancient seas. These date from the Silurian era of about 400 million years ago and are the remains of cup-animals not unlike tiny corals. Both they and the mud of the ocean bed in which they were deposited have been turned to stone, and heaved up above the sea as rock by the earth movements of aeons ago. This dark rock is Coniston limestone, part of a thick bed running right across country from west to east, from near the coast to the head of Windermere. Unlike the limestone of the later Carboniferous era, which is white or coloured in various shades of grey, the Coniston series is a dark blue-grey, the lime content much lower than that of the lighter-coloured rock. Yet somehow, the farmers long ago found that this rock did contain lime; it too was burned in kilns to produce lime for fertilizer, house-plaster and mortar. An old, delightful lime-kiln which used Coniston limestone was built into an outcrop of it more than a hundred years ago. A ruin now, but still recognisable, it appears by the edge of the Coniston to Ambleside road on a steep bend about half a mile before the Tilberthwaite Gill turn-off.

Appletreeworth holds many surprises, particularly in the rock and mineral field, as well as that of history. Within its huge area there are fragments of the blood red ore and lovely emerald green calcite, coloured by yet another different form of iron oxide. You may find limestone turned by primeval earth heat to coarse crystals of 'sugar marble', a name which should explain itself and the off-white crystals of Heavy spar, barytes, a rock identified immediately in the hand by its very heavy weight. Pieces of sky blue azurite - a copper carbonate - have been found, together with the usual but very beautiful copper pyrites, gleaming like gold in any sunlight. The bluff-line itself - more like a steep bank where the track has been gouged out, shows details of past climate. Looking carefully, at the soil-cover, one might find a rust-coloured line, showing above a dark coffee-coloured band. The rust is limonite, or bog iron, where iron salts have been leached from the rather sandy topsoil by the wet climate of many hundreds of years ago.

Perhaps the greatest surprise is the bloomery, close to one broad woodland track. By it, there are lumps of very old slag, the remains of an ancient method of iron working which up into Elizabethan times was the method used in Furness. Many of these bloomeries date to the late Middle Ages; some even later. The Appletreeworth example is astonishing; the slag found has been quite definitely dated as pre-Roman! Which suggests a site manned by people of the true Iron Age; an era impossible to date with certainty but probably beginning in Britain about 300 B.C.

The track continues to wind through the woodland. After about half a mile, it leads off to the left, towards the beck. Here is the oldest type of bridge known, a clapper bridge, a primitive structure of slate slabs laid simply on large boulders. This example unfortunately cannot be dated, but I suspect it to be no more than a couple of centuries old and quite probably much less than that. Yet this clapper bridge, once crossed, leads one along a broad track protected by a high cobble and earth bank but crudely paved underfoot. This is often the pattern of mediaeval tracks of the 12th to 15th centuries and perhaps more work of Furness Abbey's servants. It leads up the fell to the sodden acres of Caw Moss, the watershed of the River Lickle, to join eventually the other old paved track of Walna Scar, between Coniston and Dunnerdale. At the head of the wood a wooden footbridge spans the gorge of the growing river but is lower than an obvious abutment of an arched bridge which once crossed this ravine. If this were once a pack-horse bridge, then surely, it would be unique in Cumbria? From what we can see, it would have had one very narrow arch, perched a good 30 feet above the water; a bridge, one imagines, built by skilled engineers at considerable cost. For what? Copper miners again? Of the 17th and 18th centuries? Pack-horsing the ore down through the wood as a direct route to Broughton from where, on the nearby coast, it could be shipped away? No one seems to know, and I can find no record. From the map the track which would have crossed the bridge joins a direct route north west to Ravenglass by way of the south-western slopes of Harter Fell and down into Eskdale. Almost every step of the way makes an ideal smugglers' route! It weaves across wild and little known country where smugglers could pass with the full knowledge and connivance of the inhabitants, who also kept a weather eye open for the Customs officers, people not liked and often seen as unnecessary hindrances in a thriving and widespread 'industry'.

The vanished bridge is not the only surprise here, at the end of the wood. Along the slope of the fell there are pillars of rhyolite, a light grey rock very similar to a fine-grained granite. Here it appears in the form of long hexagonal pillars tilted down into the soil and seemingly too regular in shape and form to be anything other than man-made. This tiny series, a miniature Giant's Causeway type of rock-formation is the result of a 'dyke'; a stream of molten abyssal rock forcing its way towards the surface through weaknesses in the native rock millions of years ago. Cooling slowly as it came enabled the molten material to form near-perfect angular shapes by regular and steady splitting. The same type of hexagonal cracks - but not pillars - may be seen in mud drying in the sunlight, or on roads stressed by severe frost. The pillars of this Appletreeworth material were formed below ground, but eventually, the rhyolite (a word which means, in rough translation, the rock which flows) was slowly exposed to the open air by continued weathering and erosion of the top cover. These pillars, row after row of them, and all uncannily hexagonal, appear in several places in this area, one magnificent set marking the ravine of Torver Beck, a stream flowing from the slopes of the mountain above, Coniston Old Man. Here, the stream has exploited the original dyke whence came the molten rhyolite, and cut down savagely into the softer rock alongside, exposing the pillars and creating the deep stream valley. One farmer, years ago, used some of the slabs to make an intriguing stile through one of his old drystone walls, much to the amazement of many people using it today, convinced the farmer was an exceptionally skilled mason.

The woodland fauna and flora of Appletreeworth is as equally fascinating as its amazing tangle of rock and mineral, but like it, is often met or seen only after observation and sometimes, careful search. *Briza*, a grass with tiny, ball like seed heads, grows thickly along the beck bank. The seeds, quivering and nodding in the slightest breath of wind, give it the old Cumbrian name of 'Dothery grass'; *dothery* being a form of dithery. Here it appears en masse, a delightful sight in a slight breeze, with all dainty heads nodding together. It reveals where the lime content of these rocks is slowly leaching out, for Briza is generally a *calcophile* a lover and indicator of lime-rich conditions. In the more acid soil, tall spires of heath and marsh spotted orchids appear. One favoured habitat is amongst the long grass of the woodland rides where, in the wetter patches, spikes of orange yellow bog asphodel flare en masse every August.

Grey wagtails, permanent residents here and the yellow species, gloriously-hued summer immigrants from Africa, haunt the beck in season. Patient herons fish for sharp-witted, fast moving beck trout in the clear stream running swiftly by the old, ruined farm. This is a sad but lovely place, where the stones of a once delightful fell farm, close by the tinkling, hurrying beck, tumble down a little more year by year, the whole mass of the ruin growing annually; slowly and inevitably merging with great dark cushions of *Polytrichum* moss and waist-high clumps of purple moor grass. The house, still with traces of coloured plaster on the inside walls, the barns, even the old privy and little house-garden, can all be seen, but I can discover very little of who lived here and when. It was a ruin long before the Forestry Commission took over this area and covered so much of the once-bare fell with their tall, close-ranked trees.

The dark conifers, so often condemned by those disliking their solid, sullen ranks and chilly gloom beneath them, do bring some benefits. One is the goldcrest, which echoes sharp cries in the conifer fronds, the tiny bird often unseen, the sound so high-pitched that it is barely audible above the sigh of branch and bough in the wind. With luck, plus a great deal of caution, and perhaps some skill, one may glimpse roe deer which use the woods as shelter and cover in bad weather. The small, goat-like but infinitely graceful animals, are foxy-red in summer, dull brown in winter - but with glaring white backsides, better danger signals than the rabbit's tail when the deer move away in panic. Badgers are resident here; I have found their pad marks all about a wasp nest, dug from the red soil of a grassy bank, the grubs, the fat wasp larvae, gone altogether, and nothing left but a few angry and disconsolate adult insects buzzing aimlessly over the torn grass. In the clay of the same bank, frequently, the cat-like, in-line-ahead footprints of a fox appear, for it is a regular visitor to the same area. Giant dragonflies black and gold-ringed, born as grotesque larvae in the fast-running beck below, patrol the green rides between the trees, hunting down their winged insect prey with speed and deadly precision. Masses of bright-berried rowans are another speciality of this lovely woodland, a marvellous line of them marking the approach to the old bridge crossing the beck. Buzzards, riding the thermals above the trees, mew like so many squalling cats high over the valley, often annoyed by a pair of ravens which attack these solemn, staid birds like two dark-feathered, winged muggers.

Yet despite all this variety in this lovely stretch of woodland, there are several features missing which are normal to other wooded areas of Furness. The considerable number of conifers, plus the lack of broad-leafed, deciduous trees betrays at once the comparative newness of Appletreeworth as a woodland area. The Rusland woods, east and south of here, particularly towards the south end of the valley, are entirely different, revealing a much older established type of woodland.

The first thing noticeable in Rusland is the predominance of deciduous trees. Oak, hazel, beech and ash, with birch - both silver and common species - generally on the poorer, wetter land, are well represented. Conifers, often thinly scattered or single trees, are largely limited to Scots pine or larch and the gloomy yews. All of these, deciduous and otherwise, are for the most part older trees, many of them excellent specimens. They are never in obvious groups or stands, but like woodland or natural regeneration, occur as a varied series of species scattered through the whole area.

Any observant woodland walker, however, will notice one peculiarity of this place. This is the way in which there are obvious separate tall trees of various species with many smaller specimens in between which have several and sometimes many, branches sprouting from one rootstock. Far

Typical Rusland woodland - 'coppice with standards'

from being naturally regenerated woodland, old but well-looked after, it is carefully and deliberately man-made. It is, for the most part a 'coppice with standards' type, wherein standards are tall, well-spaced straight-growing timber trees and the coppice is composed of rootstocks with many branches, the result of regular cutting, the timber being a crop. Sadly, the practice has been discontinued for a long time in most places; it rarely happens today, but the trademarks of yesteryear are plain to see in these old woods.

The coppicing took place every 15 to 17 years, when the poles available from each rootstock were anything up to nine inches in diameter, and ideal for a variety of uses. In earlier times, the principal use was in the making of charcoal before this fuel for the iron and steel furnaces was ousted by the use of coke. The coppicing, now neglected, the tall standards and the mouldering, circular platforms whereon the charcoal was prepared remain - reminders of a highly skilled trade probably not much changed in method from that of the Bronze Age smiths of 4000 years ago.

In charcoal making the available timber - the coppiced wood being ideally about 6 inches in diameter - was cut into yard-long lengths. This was arranged, each piece standing vertically about a central pole called a *mottie peg*, in a circle of about 20 feet or more across. When the circle was complete, it was then covered with turf, followed by a further covering of *sammel*, which was fine-riddled earth, or sandy material found by the nearest beck. When the final covering was complete the mottie peg (always longer than the rest, and protruding well above the covering) was withdrawn and into the hole thus left, glowing charcoal was placed. The hole was sealed up and if done properly, the whole pile would smoulder and burn off the water and gases of the stacked wood to leave perfect charcoal! Unfortunately, it took about 10 tons of wood to make one ton of charcoal, so one may imagine the devastation of woodland before coke took over as fuel. Charcoal was not the only woodland product; there were the besoms or birch-twig brushes for the lawns and driveways of stately homes, woven ships' fenders of the same material and a tremendous lot of birch cut to supply the bobbin trade. In the early 19th century bobbin mills appeared in almost every southern Lakeland valley where wood was available and water-power nearby.

Another woodland product, of which the traces are rather rare, was oak bark, used extensively in tanning leather. It is still used today, but in much less quantity and not locally. It was a job which produced the Furness surname of "Barker", still very common in the district today. The traces of this trade in the woods linger on in the remains of the barkers' hut, though these are now very few. The huts were stone-based, with a neat fireplace and sometimes a crudely flagged floor. The roof of timber and bracken or turf thatch has long gone, but the stone base remains. Charcoalers sometimes built similar huts but generally theirs were temporary and often lacked the stone base.

What a marvellous time for the children of these workers! High summer spent in the woods; hard work, and plenty of it, but so much to see and listen to in the leafy woods, from a cock pheasant's staccato call to the hoo-hooing of lovesick wood-pigeons and the shrill cries of the green woodpecker foretelling, they would say, the arrival of more rain. The charcoalers dreaded the rain, for 'first the wind, and then the rain' and the wind was a prime enemy. Finding any cracks or holes in the covering of wood being burned for charcoal, it could fan the smouldering mass into flame, so that the whole lot would blaze. This meant that the charcoaler, if he did not do something about it right away, such as sealing any crack with earth or damping the lot down with water, would end up with nothing but a giant heap of ashes.

It is a great pity that the general coppicing of woodland has fallen into disuse. The charcoaling, except for a few enthusiasts and with very limited use, has gone for good, but the woodlands could still produce a regular crop. Regular 'coppicing with standards' is the way to preserve our native Furness woodlands. At the same time, it would conserve much of the wildlife, big and small, flora and fauna together. By careful woodland 'farming' of such areas, we would have, always, one part of maturing, standing woodland, with other sections in various stages reaching towards that. The timber could be used for many purposes other than in obsolete charcoal making and there would be cover, food and shelter for a host of wildlife living in an area of varied timber growth.

In the Rusland valley the famous beeches, once over 100 in number, but reduced by age and sickness, line one side of the valley road under the lee of tall Yew Crag (see frontispiece). In autumn and winter the copper-coloured leaf carpet under these old and lovely trees is a sure attraction for all sorts of birds and animals: blue, great and coal tits, chaffinches and their northern visitors and look-a-likes, the bramblings; woodmice, red squirrels, and deer all love beechmast, hard but much sought-after seeds, nutritious and rich in oil, but held within prickly seed cases.

Deer tracks, of red and roe, wind through the trees and in former days, the roe and the red would lie up overnight under the yews. Too much disturbance and too many greedy and stupid people and poachers have stopped that and now the deer are much more furtive and keep well away from any road or the taint of human scent. The same uncaring people have made the grotesque hawfinches (with beaks which crack wild cherry stones as if they were peanut shells) grow very cautious indeed. They are present in the valley but difficult to find and watch. Not so the red squirrels; I have had a trio of them playing about over my head in a January snowstorm close by the road (No. They do *not* hibernate!), a crowd of hungry bullfinches pulling at ash keys in front of me and marsh tits flitting through holly and hawthorn undergrowth almost at my feet, all at one and the same time. At other times I have watched a lovely 'silktail', that beautiful but erratic winter visitor, the waxwing, on the blackthorns and leaving to seek shelter under the trees.

I once fell over a red stag, a true royal with crowns - a trio of points at the end of his antlers - sitting out a heavy downpour under the trees. He was oblivious of my approach upwind of him (as I was of his presence) due to the tremendous noise of the rain. It was a meeting which caused great fright to both stag and human! The inexperienced are unlikely to go very far in these woods without the jays - most watchful and cunning of the clever crow family - shouting a warning to all and sundry. Yet even for the clumsiest there is so much to see and hear (and smell when the bluebells are out) in these lovely old woods.

One 'flower' of autumn is Fly Agaric, that beautiful scarlet, white-spotted and poisonous fungi which was once so often shown on the cover of childrens' books of fairy stories - an astonishing place on which to portray something so dangerous. But though harmful to humans, Agaric is eaten by slugs and nibbled by rabbits without obvious harm. The danger to humans lies in the muscarine held within it; this is a halucogen, producing effects which are very similar and equally as dangerous as L.S.D., a toxic and erratic drug. In old Russia, muscarine from the Agaric was known as a 'Catherine', because it was supposedly a tipple of Catherine the Great, but any experimenters of today should be warned. This fungus may kill and even if the subject survives, there is no telling when the same wild symptoms may recur, hours, weeks, or months later, and all without warning!

This lovely valley, 'Rolf's land', was once the possession of some long dead and now unknown early mediaeval squire. Rusland Hall, built on a knoll in the valley centre, is certainly a very old site. It belonged to the Rawlinson family as far back as 1574. One member of it, Captain Rawlinson, who raised his own troop of horse, was at the Battle of Marston Moor in July 1644, during the Civil War, fighting on the Parliamentary side, when the Royalists were soundly defeated. He was also the man responsible for working the iron forge in the hamlet of Force Forge; a decidedly pretty hamlet, full of the sound of running water from the pounding waterfalls and not so far away from the Hall in the same valley. The furnace was an attempt at bringing the valley into the world of industry, for as recorded, '....there are no mines at work in the parish, nor are any minerals found there, except some fine specimens of copper ore, which are picked up occasionally near the brooks in Rusland...'.

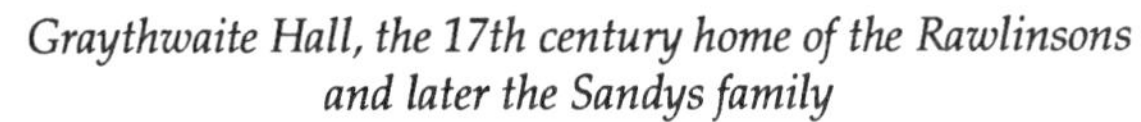
Graythwaite Hall, the 17th century home of the Rawlinsons and later the Sandys family

This was a report which seems to have started off the story of the Rusland coiners. The Rawlinsons had a hand in the extensive copper mines of Greenburn in Little Langdale and according to the story, this was worked at least in part by German miners. They were so impressed by the quality of the copper ore that they hit upon the idea of making 'golden' guineas from it and promptly and secretly proceeded to do so with the connivance of their employer. Unfortunately during a dance at Hawkshead, a dancing miner's pocket burst open, scattering his collection of 'guineas' over the dance floor. News of this sped around the valley and reached the ears of the authorities who decided to investigate. Such news travelled fast, but the report of Government officers coming to investigate travelled even faster. At Rusland Hall, the squire was away so the initiative was left in the hands of his wife. According to the tale, she took the remaining minted coins and the coining presses and plant, and threw them into the peat hags of Rusland Pool, the great marsh which spread across the floor of the valley. Where - sunk deep in the peat, again according to the tale - they are still!

There is more tangible evidence of another industry (which was perfectly legal) on the west side of the valley at Black Beck. This was a gunpowder works established in 1862, now replaced by a caravan site, but with relict walls and buildings still to be seen. It was a hazardous trade in which explosions occurred from time to time. One serious accident happened in 1868, when nine workers were killed outright; another six years later, harmed no one. Even so, it is not surprising that amongst the housewives of nearby Bouth, it was the practice always to have clean sheets on the bed because, as the housewives said, 'We never knew when the men would come home from the works dead or injured'.

A less obvious reminder of these works can be found growing in the valley nearby. This is a bush, glossy leaved, in fruit with berries which may be black, red, or green on the same spray. The bush is alder buckthorn, and charcoal made from it was particularly useful in World War II, when it was used in the fuses of Mills hand grenades. The buckthorn charcoal burns at an extremely steady rate, which is very important, obviously, when reliable time fuses are essential. Alder buckthorn also has a gentler use; it is the foodplant of the lovely sulpher-coloured brimstone butterfly; in Cumbria, this lovely lepidopteran is now scarce and highly localised.

'Crow Hall', the nickname for the Quaker Meeting House at Rook How, is also on the west side of the valley. Built in 1725, with seating for about 150 people, it was meant more as a general assembly room for the Quakers in the district rather than as a separate Meeting House for one specific area. Mellowed by time, close by the roadside, but half-shrouded in trees, it is a delightful building, which like so many of the dales cottages and houses, seems to have evolved - to have grown slowly from the ground rather than been built by human hands! One might also say the same for Rusland church, which is built high on a rock towards the northern end of the valley. There is a wonderful view of the southern Rusland valley from the churchyard, a place which holds the ashes of Arthur Ransome. Not only was he the author of a well-loved series of childrens' books, the most famous perhaps being *Swallows and Amazons*, set in background which was a kind of hybrid between Windermere and Coniston Water; but an important war correspondent for the *Manchester Guardian* in Russia during the Revolution, and a personal friend of Lenin from the very start of that tremendous time. Ransome's gravestone, and that of his Russian wife, lie at the eastern end of the churchyard under an enormous windblown Scots pine.

East of the quiet Rusland valley there are more woods, particularly on the eastern shore of Coniston Water. One delightful woodland is just beyond the hamlet of Nibthwaite, at the edge of a bay not far from Peel Island. Here, more fungi appear in old and formerly coppiced woodland. These strange growths may include the ominously named Death Cap - seemingly an innocuous, pallid mushroom, yet one more deadly than a cobra bite - eaten, it has similar effect, destroying red blood cells and paralysing muscle, causing certain death if not treated within 24 hours. Then there is the Destroying Angel, also deadly, which looks like a shelled, hard-boiled egg as it peeps through the leaf mould in much the same place. It sounds very dangerous and it is; but only to the deliberately stupid and foolhardy, for both of these poisonous fungi grow away from the usual casual tourist haunts. They are found only by careful search, and usually by mycologists, or those realising their danger and respecting it.

The woods nearer the lake are often crowded with various species of more innocuous fungi in September, most of them being completely harmless, though many appear exotic or bizarre in shape, form or colour. They range from fungi with caps big enough to use as a hat, bright yellow growths like broccoli, red topped 'mushrooms', appropriately nicknamed 'sickeners' and which certainly make one violently sick if eaten - though surely only a fool would attempt that - and the stinkhorn, which as its name implies, has rather a strong smell.

This last is a really weird beauty; beauty because once the cap and stalk is first clear of any cover, it seems to be made of thinnest, whitest, lightest lace or modern, feather-light polystyrene, with a head of pure white cotton lace. Before that stage however, the cap is covered with bright green slime,

Above: Furness Abbey
Below: Tilberthwaite

Victorian lighthouse at Rampside

smelling, at first, like violets, but rapidly changing to that of a dead elephant! The smell of rotten meat attracts greenbottles, those beautiful metallic, brilliant emerald green flies, cousin to the bluebottle, also a lover of dead meat! The clustering flies eat the slime, which contains the fungal spores and fly away. When they void the spores, which are unharmed even after passing through the fly's gut, these "seeds" fall to the ground to grow and throw out mycelia. These dead-white 'roots' thread through the soil, budding off at intervals into spherical 'witches eggs'; young stinkhorns which elongate and mature into the adult fungus very quickly indeed. The stinkhorn is a fascinating fungus; but one which may never pass unnoticed, even to those with no more than the slightest sense of smell!

Where else to go in woodland? The obvious answer is Grizedale Forest, all eight thousand and more acres of it, covering the head of the Rusland valley in its glorious, tree-clothed sprawl. This place is organised; it has a visitors' centre, and a marvellous diaorama explaining the work of the forester as well as showing the rich wildlife found within these woods. It has mapped-out and marked walks, a tree-top roost where one may stay overnight, and wake early to see red or roe deer feeding almost at one's feet. Altogether, Grizedale is a huge area where one may wander at will, a place where scores of walks and tracks may be explored without hindrance of any kind provided the Country Code, which is nothing more than common sense exemplified, is always observed.

This forest is well organised and well staffed by helpful people knowing their business. There are, however, plenty of smaller inlets to the woods, and these are my preference. For one thing, they are generally more remote, away from the tourist routes and for another, they are quieter and give one perhaps a better chance of seeing some of the wild life. Bogle Crag, in Rusland, is such a place; with deciduous woods on one side, and conifer the other. There is a rattling, clear-watered stream and great slabs of rock, bearing the scratches of ice-travel of thousands of years ago, rearing up between acres of Norwegian spruce and Western red cedar. There are squirrels to be seen, goldcrests to listen to as well as jays, woodpigeons, woodpeckers and many more. Tracks of roe and red deer can be found and followed; even, with wind and weather right, lots of peace and quiet, and a whole load of luck, the deer themselves to be seen and enjoyed. There are the ancient pitsteads of long-dead charcoalers to be found together with the remains of ancient huts - even one used by people burning green bracken years ago. This was for the soap trade of Kendal. Green bracken was burned, producing ashes rich in potash. Mixed with water, these form a strong alkali, called *lye;* and this solution, boiled with animal fat, made a crude but effective soap. When Kendal was in its prime as a centre of the woollen industry, such soap was very much in demand to clean the wool.

These woodlands of the south are wonderful places for children as well as adults still young enough in heart and mind to use their senses to the full. Even the vicinity of the formal car park of Bogle Crag is interesting; immediately above it, at the edge of the road up into the trees, there are white and pale pink berried rowan trees; these are specimens of the Hupeh Rowan first brought into this country as recently as 1910 from Western China. In the 'backend', the autumn, white-and-pale-pink berried, red and purple-leaved, this graceful tree, scarce bigger than a bush, is both bizarre and beautiful. It seems fitting advertisement, or challenge, to those who love the woodlands.

10: White Rock, Grey Church

BEFORE THE FATEFUL year of 1974, when the county of Cumbria first came into existence, all that part of Lancashire north of Morecambe Bay was known as 'Lancashire North of the Sands', a graphic and self-explanatory title. In all that area, there is only one true sea-cliff - Humphrey Head, which juts out into the mud and sand of the 'Bay not far from the ancient and strangely-named village of Flookburgh. On the map, the outline of the Head looks rather like a jagged tooth, a sharp-tipped fang on the eastern edge of the broader Cartmel peninsula. Of near-white, steel-hard carboniferous limestone, it rears over 160 feet above the sand, tailing off seawards to a low ridge of stark, uptilted rock splashed with the brilliant orange lichen, *Xanthoria* (which means 'the Golden One'!) and dark patches of *Verrucaria maura*, commonly known as 'Tar-spot'; another lichen which

Humphrey Head. The limestone headland near Flookburgh has been called the 'Box Hill of the North' because of its wide variety of flora

survives and thrives at tide-level.

In high summer Humphrey Head and the shore at its foot, is a popular rendezvous, particularly with families from present day south Lancashire. At its best in this high season the wild flowers of the Head and those growing in the woods below it reveal a startling variety of species. Under the trees, particularly where the woodland fringes the narrow road, a striking plant grows in the shadows. Considering the dark nature given it the shady woods would seem an appropriate habitat for it is *Belladonna,* sometimes better known as Deadly nightshade. The scientific title is *Atropa belladonna Atropa* from the deadly alkaloid *atropine* found within every part of the plant; root, leaf, stalk, flower and fruit. Five of the luscious black berries, like enormous and glossy cherries, will certainly kill an adult; three would make a child very ill. Fortunately, these fruits have an unappetising, vapid taste unlikely to be relished, even by the ignorant and foolhardy.

Why Belladonna? Amongst other things, atropine, used as eye-drops, relaxes the ocular muscles enlarging and beautifying the eye-pupils. In Renaissance Italy, women used it as a cosmetic, and though it certainly enhanced the eyes of these dark beauties, it would, for a time, make them unable to focus on anything! Atropine is still used in opthalmology today, yet despite such bizarre and dangerous properties, it is full cousin to the humbler potato. Belladonna thrives in shade, producing dark-veined, flesh-coloured flowers and visited frequently by bumble bees which seem, like the rabbits which eat the poisonous leaves with apparent impunity, to be completely unaffected by the plant's deadly poison.

Humphrey Head, because of its rich and varied flora, unique even in this lovely area, has been called the 'Box Hill of the North', Box Hill, in Surrey, is noted for its immense variety of chalk and lime-loving wild flowers. Like its southern counterpart, the Head also bristles with rare and unusual plant species. Spiked speedwell, a tall cone of brightest, purest blue, grows here; so does the dainty Maidenhair fern - if you can find it! Rock samphire (*Crithmum maritimum),* blooms in crack and crevice. Now a protected rarity in Britain, it was formerly used in making a delicious sauce, being collected from Beachy Head and other hazardous southern cliffs for the demanding markets of old London, particularly in Elizabethan times. It is noted by Shakespeare, these lines appearing in *King Lear:*

'How fearful
And dizzy tis to cast one's eyes so low!
The crows and choughs that wing the midway air
Show scarce so gross as beetles; halfway down
Hangs one that gathers samphire, dreadful trade!'

Bunches of red stemmed Pellitory of the Wall (described on the walls of Gleaston Castle. See Chapter 5) drape the tall western flank of the Head. Small-leaved lime, (an ancient resident), wind-tossed hawthorn, and pale-barked ash drape the slopes or struggle up into the wind. On the clitter, which is sliding, flat-sided limestone scree, dark yews cling for a roothold, glooming the woodland and bearing, on some, perhaps the most beautiful of all British fungi. This is the Sulphur polypore (*Laetporus sulphureus*), a fungal parasite; a species which crippled some of the ships of Nelson's navy even as they lay on the stocks long before launching. A century before that, the same species attacked and devastated the oak timbers of the *Speedwell*, sister ship to the renowned *Mayflower* which took the Pilgrim Fathers to the New World to escape persistent religious persecution in England and the rest of western Europe. *Speedwell* should have crossed the Atlantic in 1620 with the *Mayflower*, but the fungal-ridden timbers of the first vessel forbade any such voyage, and the founding fathers of America sailed alone on her sister vessel.

To those with a love of wild flowers, Humphrey Head, in June, July and August, is unique. The floral pageant of summer is sheer delight but of all the attractions, the creamy-flowered Dropwort, (*Filipendula vulgaris*) is my favourite. Blooming in late July and August, it whitens the long grass of the Head's windblown top, the small, ball-like flowers nodding with every breath of wind amongst a host of near-blond Briza, the constantly quivering Dothery grass of old Cumberland. Related to the meadowsweet, but with each bloom no more than faintly sweet-smelling, unlike its bigger, brasher and more obvious cousin, these massed Dropwort blooms, sun-warmed and scented, perfume every whiff of wind from the sea.

The flattened stones of the beach, far below, and the mud and sand of this small bay under the headland are busy with human visitor in the holiday season. Not so very long ago, they were busier still, with people coming from near and far to take the waters of the famous mineral spring; the so-called Holy Well, which still flows from beneath the trees almost on the tide line. Now, it is difficult to find and when found, hard to realise its past interest and importance. Disgracefully, the beach about the source has been bulldozed flat; the spring water, ignored and unlabelled, now rarely noticed by any visitors, trickles from a small, insignificant plastic pipe onto mud fouled all too often by man-made rubbish. It was not always so; in the early 19th century, the mineral water was sold from a fisherman's cottage (now gone without trace) on the foreshore, close by the valued Holy Well. The scene presented there in those times was dramatically described by a visitor in the 1840s:

> 'The cottage adjoining the well was inhabited by a fisherman's numerous family, who lived on the first floor, under which, in a dark, black-looking kitchen, there was a small iron boiler, filled with spa water and heated by turf and peat from the nearby mosses.
>
> Sometimes the ancient dame, with two generations at least in attendance,... used a black cauldron, upon a hearth fire, instead of the boiler....then, with her dark countenance in that gloomy apartment, her dishevelled locks floating over her disordered attire, she looked like a witch of former days, dispensing her portions to 20 or 30 horsemen crowding round her dirty door... .
>
> She sat down on a three-legged stool, by the embers of the hearth fire, wearing a linsey-wool lower garment and a semi kind of gown reaching only to the hips, with short, wide sleeves, which left bare her once-muscular but now shrivelled arms, one of which she leaned akimbo on her knee....in her right hand she held a tobacco pipe about four inches long, and black with 40 year's usage, and which she smoked vehemently at every short interval of her tale....the one window was in a corner, its few panes nearly all stuffed with rags, but a gleam or two from the burning turf would occasionally irradiate this almost dark apartment..'.

When the house fell into disrepair, which was inevitable, for it was built too near the encroaching tides for safety and comfort, the precious liquid was dispensed from a small wooden hut little bigger than a large wardrobe; the charge was twopence a cup. Later still, the clear water ran into an earthen sink, and was taken up, free, by eager visitors. Long before the railway came, wooden barrels full of spa-water lurched across the dangerous sands of Morecambe Bay between the threat of the twice-daily tides, carried either on pack ponies or light carts. Much of this barrelled liquid went to Heysham Head, and was marketed there as something of a cure-all, a panacea to the growing number of holidaymakers. In the latter half of the 19th century, with the arrival of the railway, the spa-water was collected into metal milk churns and went direct by train to Morecambe, selling at sixpence a glass in that increasingly popular resort.

Though commonly known for many years as the Holy Well, it was neither sanctified nor patronised officially by the church, even though it was eagerly sought by a large cross-section of local people and visitors from afar. One group which came a long way were the lead miners of Alston and district. The Alston lead miners came here by the dozen for many years. '.....they rode all the way on the little mountain Galloways (ponies)...' reads

An old print of Humphrey Head showing the cottage by the well - long since disappeared

one account '...quartered themselves in the neighbouring villages, bathed in the sea, and drank the (spa) waters in quantity... a gallon a day sometimes'. The Alston miners returned to the Humphrey Head spa for forty years in succession and all the miners appear to have believed in the water's medicinal value; their stories of its wonderful properties losing nothing in the telling. In analysis, the spa water is surprisingly similar to that of Wiesbaden in Germany which, unlike Humphrey Head, was renowned throughout western Europe. The lesser-known Cartmel spring water, much more localised in its fame, was reputedly a positive cure for the 'stone, gout, and cutaneous diseases' in its late Georgian and early Victorian prime.

What is the truth? Is it medicinally useful? Analysts and medical men say it is nothing more than a mild laxative containing sodium chloride, sulphate of lime and magnesium chloride in ratios of 41 to 11 to 5; a sort of Epsom salts dissolved from some subterranean deposit deep in the hard limestone.

The cubicle from which the water was dispensed at the Holy Well. The water was drawn from a trough at the back. Nothing remains now of the well except a muddy trickle

Truth being stranger than fiction, however, it is now believed that such spa water may have much more value than was formerly thought. Surprisingly, it was research into the weightlessness problems encountered by American astronauts which encouraged re-investigation. The astronauts were immersed in water for long periods of time and it was found that this increased urine flow considerably. Two hundred years ago, a brilliant 18th century doctor, investigating the lead-poisoning of Devonshire cider drinkers (the cider being brewed and stored in lead vessels) showed the way, for he discovered that such immersion, by increasing urine flow, greatly alleviated the lead poisoning of the cider drinkers. Is this what happened to the Alston miners? Did their frequent sea bathing, coupled with copious draughts of spa water flush the lead from their systems, and bring obvious relief? It would seem a strong possibility. Today, with advanced medical techniques and better working conditions, such industrial poisoning is usually kept in check. Very few people ever drink the Humphrey Head spa water these days, though at least one person has used the rather salty/bitter liquid in wine-making! Though the water is harmless, it is surely not a practice to be recommended?

Other than the summer floral delights, the sweeping limestone cliff, and the fascination of the Holy Well, this area has other delights on offer. Few visitors ever bother to explore the gravelly shore to the west of the Head. Here, the shoreline curves round in a neat sweep towards Flookburgh, passing some strange rock formations. These are small *mesas,* which is a Spanish word often used by geologists and here meaning tables of rock, like those huge flat-topped formations which appear in so many Western films.

A brockram mesa near Flookburgh

These local examples are much smaller, more ill-formed and far less dramatic than their North American counterparts. They are composed of small but interesting lumps of stone called *brockram* by the lead miners of the north-east; a mixture, a fossilised jumble of desert sandstone, limestone, and broken fossils. It is a common rock formation in the Eden Valley and much of old Kirkby Stephen is built of it. Over here, in the southwest of the county, it is a rarity.

To examine this rock is to look back into geological history and the physical conditions, including weather, of more than 130 millions years ago. The sandstone, for example, is an unusual type; a rich, sunbaked red-brown, with each and every sand grain forming it bearing the betraying scratches of windblown desert sand rather than that from shoreline or estuary. Examined under a low powered microscope, the grains appear as classical examples of the geologist's 'millet seed sand', each grain being rounded into seed-like form. Shaped thus by harsh desert winds of long ago, each 'seed' has a pellicle or skin of iron oxide, formed by long desert weathering. The minute scratches on this betray countless collisions against neighbouring particles, all being driven continually together by winds blowing over a barren desert of the Permian era; a scorching, sun-blasted, waterless inferno of 130 or more million years ago - give or take a few million years either way!

The limestone within the brockram is older still and rich in annular (ringed) fossils; these are called 'St. Cuthbert's beads' because of their ring-like shape. Some, in Victorian times, were made into simple, stony necklaces, each circle a stalk-ring from an extinct and fossilized species of Sea-pen, a static marine worm with feathery, plume-like gills and filters. Now extinct, it swarmed on the muddy bed of a warm and shallow tropical sea about 300 million years ago.

What of brockram itself? It was formed by the rare flash-floods, caused by violent, torrential rainstorms, occurring with gaps of many years between them, perhaps even of centuries, in that desert inferno. Bounding flood-water, bearing masses of desert sand and other material in loose suspension, tore across a Permian desert, roared over a limestone escarpment, (itself thrust up from the sea bed by earth movement aeons before), and poured over flatter land below in a myriad braided shallow channels. Such floods, by their very nature, ceased very quickly, the water sinking rapidly into the parched sand, but leaving behind the temporary channels crammed with a jumble of desert sand, limestone scree particles and limestone fossils ripped from the escarpment. Fossilized to rock over the years by long burial and earth pressure, the brockram strata formed has been exposed by weathering and eroded by the sea, into these attractive mesas dotting the beach west of Humphrey Head. As already explained, few people know of their existence, fewer still are driven by curiosity to explore this fascinating section of shore. Soon, possibly within a decade or two, these mesas will be gone, for relentless and powerful marine erosion of this comparatively soft rock continues with each and every tide.

The narrow lane from Humphrey Head leads north and west towards the village of Flookburgh, the grey ribbon of road winding and twisting through flat green fields which not too long ago were marshland or shore. This road marks the Cartmel end of an ancient and once principal ford across the 'Bay from Hest Bank, north of Lancaster. It passes Wraysholme Tower, a 15th century pele, a miniature fortress, built to guard the Cartmel end of the Oversands ford immediately after the bloody Wars of the Roses. In the hands of the Stanleys, whose forces swung the Battle of Bosworth in the Lancastrians' favour and ensured the death of Richard III, it was a stronghold guarding a key ford for the House of Lancaster over Morecambe Bay sands to Lancaster and the south. It was made specifically to warn of, rather than prevent, any surprise movement or attack across the sands by any remaining members of the Yorkist faction (of which there were many in the north) against the allies and supporters of the new king, Henry VII, first of the Tudor monarchy.

Originally, Wraysholme was a favoured house of the Harringtons, Lord of Aldingham, owners of much land in the Cartmel area, and incidentally fervent supporters of the Yorkist cause. A father and son of this family were killed together by the Lancastrians at the Battle of Wakefield during the selfsame Wars of the Roses, when their Cartmel home was then little more than a semi-fortified country house. It became a true tower house, a pele-type fortress, when the present tower was built in 1485, a significant year, the time of the defeat of Richard III at Bosworth Field, when Wraysholme and the Cartmel lands were the gift of the grateful Henry Tudor for the Stanley's help in that grim, treacherous, and bloody affair.

Wraysholme was no more than two years old when another Yorkist came by. The ten year old Pretender Lambert Simnel and his mix of forces probably marched this way after landing at Piel. The Yorkist band came east and south in a desperate, last-fling challenge to the new king. The defeat of this army at Stoke Field near Nottingham a few days later finally ended the long drawn out conflict of the Wars of the Roses in favour of the Lancastrian Henry Tudor.

There is no record of any of the Stanleys of Wraysholme attempting to stop or slow down the Yorkists, (who would have overwhelmed them in any case, by sheer force of numbers); nor can I find any record proving Wraysholme involvement in any way with a 'Bay crossing of Lambert Simnel and his forces. Simnel's army may well have gone inland, ignoring Wraysholme ford and taken a longer (but much less dangerous) route clear of any 'Bay crossing. They could have travelled east, over the fells to Kendal and passed beyond, into the Yorkshire dales, before finally turning south towards the Midlands. There appears to be no full or current record of the progress of this raggle-taggle army's progress towards its final, bloody defeat near Nottingham.

Leading away from Wraysholme towards Flookburgh village, the road in early summer is delightful. Honeysuckle and wild briar drape the hedges; the deep roadside ditches are full of bright yellow flag, or blue forget-me-nots, and purple mint, the clear water often black with late tadpole swarms. Huge dragonflies hawk over the surface or patrol the narrow grey ribbon of the road. Further on still the nets, carts, and parked tractors outside some of the houses nearer the sea betray the Flookburgh shrimp fishermen. Once, this village was a prosperous little market town, helped considerably by the continuous oversands traffic in both directions between Ulverston and Lancaster. It was in the middle of a thriving trade-route which vanished almost overnight with the coming of the railways in 1855. However busy, Flookburgh was never much more than a long, house-lined single street (though ever under threat of development) and is still very small. As proof of antiquity, several of the present-day cottages bear 17th century datestones. Most of these post-date the terrible fire of 1686, when much of the village was devastated. Westward, the main street leads into another arm of Morecambe Bay, at Sandgate, where travellers of long ago took the ford west over to Ulverston; people of many kinds passing over the treacherous Cartmel sands between each and every day-time tide.

Flookburgh first had a charter given it by the younger son of Bolingbroke, Henry IV, early in the 15th century. It was a document containing rights which were reaffirmed more than two and a half centuries later, in 1663, by the Merry Monarch, Charles II. Today, the village has several pieces of regalia, including a long-handled halberd, which may well date from that time. The 17th century charter allowed the inhabitants of Flookburgh to '...hold a market upon Tuesday every week... and also a fair yearly and every year to continue at the same place... for three days... upon the morrow of the nativity of St John the Baptist... and one other fair yearly...to continue for three days upon the morrow of the feast of Saint Michael the Archangel...'. Sadly, as with so many other small places, the weekly market and the annual fair have long fallen into disuse.

The name of the village, Flookburgh, is a puzzle and the source of much argument. In 1246 it was Flokeburg, and almost 150 years later, in 1394, it had changed to Flokesburgh or Flokeberew. By the early 16th century it was close to the modern name as Flokeburgh and by 1537 closer still as Fluckburgh. So what do these titles mean? There are three possibilities. The modern suffix of *burgh* comes from the old English *burh,* which means a fortified place. The *Flook* may be from the old Norse personal name of *Floki* (mixed Saxon and Norse names are common on the west coast), so that the village may have started off as a fortified house of a recently arrived Norseman in about 900 to 1000 A.D. Unfortunately, *floki,* which in the same old tongue also means a flatfish, may be an allusion to a flat area, which is certainly true of this village built near the sea. The third possibility is that Flookburgh is named after the *fluke,* the northern name for a flatfish better known elsewhere in England as the flounder, *Platichthys flesus,* the principal fish caught in much of Morecambe Bay. Most Flookburgh folk believe this last is the most likely and as if to emphasise this the weather vane on the Victorian church, a gift of the Cavendishes of nearby Holker Hall, is fashioned into a crude representation of that strange little fish.

Though flukes are still caught in the net-lines, the favoured and more profitable prey of the Flookburgh fishermen is the shrimp, netted in the waters of receding tides, and boiled, skinned and prepared for distribution far beyond in the spotless preparation sheds of the village fishermen. Not so very long ago sturdy, thick-legged horses pulled the shrimp carts from which the fine-meshed shrimping nets were suspended; thankfully (from the shrimper's point of view) equally sturdy Diesel tractors have taken over the job. No more drying down weary horses or, as some of the ancient old village salts used to do, treating the horses' legs (or their own!) with oil rendered down from porpoise or dolphin blubber - an old remedy for arthritic joints. Modern conditions may be better in many ways, but the hardy shrimpers (whose numbers shrink as more and more leave the job) must still follow every tide in season, whatever the weather, if they are to make a reasonable living. Cockles are also taken for the market from between the tides sand; being filter feeders, they sieve plankton from the twice daily tides. The gleaming white shells are raked from the sand by the hundred and quickly gathered up.

Today, even with the usual influx of 'offcomes', Flookburgh is a quiet place, but in the past it was sorely afflicted; Robert the Bruce and his followers burnt it to the ground in the early 14th century. In both the 16th and 17th centuries plague arrived and killed off a lot of the villagers. In the closing years of the 17th century a devastating fire burnt the heart out of the village. In this last catastrophe of 1686, no less than 22 houses (plus many barns and stables) were burned down in the main thoroughfare, Market Street, causing heavy losses in '...household goods, corne, graine, maulte, bedinge, bedsteads and other goods.....to the value of three thousands pounds ...', a vast sum in those days. Number 32 Market Street, commonly called the Manor House, is a lovely old building complete with mullioned windows and a huge and decorative Yorkshire lintel over the front door. It is either a lucky escapee from the fire or more probably, a rebuild after the disaster. Opposite are two pubs, built specifically to cater for the Alston miners of the last century, who came here to take the waters at the Holy Well, on the shore under Humphrey Head. Quite probably, the delightful old Manor House was once the home of succeeding stewards of the manor. A cottage in the same street, towards Sandgate is dated 1654, but has suffered alteration, some of it possibly due to repair after the fire of long ago.

Flookburgh village is close to another settlement, Cark, often classed in local estate agency advertisement as '..a desirable place of residence'. Which means, that with more development - very often nothing more than increased house building - the two villages will come even closer together and inevitably, merge as one. Like Flookburgh, Cark (or to give it the full title, Cark-in-Cartmel) is an ancient settlement, though unlike Flookburgh, which was more concerned with Morecambe Bay fishing, Cark was embroiled in the Industrial Revolution. Here, in the 18th and 19th centuries, there was a huge cotton mill, corn mills and shipyard on Cark Beck building vessels for the Baltic timber trade or the transport of West Indian rum and sugar. There is little trace of any of this these days, but the *Engine Inn* is a reminder of much busier times. The title of the pub remembers that period, and also marks a startling series of 18th century fraud, industrial espionage, and the sly copying of patents! The engine of the inn title was a steam engine, a poor copy of a beam engine invented, developed, and finally patented by the great James Watt. The Cark copy, unlike Watt's magnificent original, failed miserably; but it took a disguised Scots engineer acting as an industrial spy, plus much litigation, before the whole sordid business was finally settled. The giant cotton mill, unfortunately, was destroyed by fire earlier this century; the water-powered corn mill ceased work years ago, but the site and some buildings still exist. The *Engine Inn* is a constant reminder, and so is the row of neat cottages by the beck, which were once occupied by the spinners of the Cark cotton mill.

Cark Hall, over to the west, is Elizabethan. Once it was home to a man who was in turn an ardent Royalist, 'popish Catholic recusant', erudite Anglo-Saxon scholar and cruel persecutor of all Quakers, including their

Cark Hall, where George Fox was imprisoned before his trial at Lancaster

great leader, George Fox. One Quaker, imprisoned with Fox in Cark Hall was cruelly and cold-bloodedly murdered by the 'Carter' - the official guide of the Oversands route - acting under the authority of Rawlinson of Cark Hall.

This happened in 1660 when the guide, whose name was Thomas Carter, was conducting a party of some 30 men on foot and horseback, across the treacherous channels and fords of the winding River Kent where it flows over the Morecambe Bay sands. Both George Fox and a Quaker from Underbarrow, near Kendal, called Miles Hubbersty - virtually a local man, which makes the crime even worse - were under guard by men who would not allow Fox to ride his own horse until they came to a place in the river channel then called Carter Ford. Only then was he allowed to mount and be led through the deep water. At this moment, according to Fox, Miles Hubbersty was '...destroyed by a wilful, wicked man... the Carter... who claped his hook in his cloak and drew him from the friends near 100 yards, so that he was strangled and drowned...'. Thomas Carter died the following year, which would please Fox immensely, for he was human enough to be a firm believer in the wrath of the Lord descending on those who persecuted him and his followers!

Cark, little more than a cluster of houses scattered about the Elizabethan Hall was never as important as Cartmel, a couple of miles further inland. Then, as now, Cartmel is usually much busier than either Cark or Flookburgh. Nowadays, the Cartmel visitors are often tourists, arriving by car. More than a century ago many would be travellers moving north and inland from the 'Bay, or those using the oversands route between Hest Bank and Ulverston, but diverting to Cartmel en route. Dominated by its huge, cathedral-sized church, the more 'up-market' Cartmel was once an important focal point and sometimes halfway-house for the better-off traveller using the treacherous route across Morecambe Bay. An old milestone near the Cartmel crossroads still points to the Oversands route but today, fortunately, few take heed unless they be accompanied by the sand-pilot, the official guide over the Sands who is still appointed by the Duchy of Lancaster.

Which is as it should be. The sheep-clipped Priory churchyard holds the bones of many a traveller drowned by the treacherous waters of Morecambe Bay. In 300 years, between about 1580 and 1880, at least 140 people suffered in this way and were entered in the burial records of Cartmel Priory. The records make sad reading, as the following examples show:

> '1687: Christopher Harrys, draper, of Cartmell.. his horse faltered and cast his load, which he endeavoured to put right....he was so long that the flood came and he was drowned..he would not call for assistance notwithstanding several came by and saw him.. .
>
> 1769: A cockle fisherman, his wife, and two grown-up daughters were crossing the sands when a thick fog came on... the cockler left the cart to try and find the way back to shore...the women were overtaken by the tide, but they let the horse have is head... the mother was washed off the cart and drowned, but the daughters were saved, the horse wading and swimming to the shore... .
>
> 1803: Thomas Warbrick drowned in crossing the sands. He and another young gentleman were going to Allithwaite (near Kents Bank) in a gig when they missed the ford; the gig overturned...Warbrick was drowned, the other man swimming to shore.
>
> 1808: A man named Walling was crossing with a horse and cart; the wheels got stuck in a quicksand, the man escaped but the horse was drowned... .
>
> 1821: A chaise returning to Ulverston with driver and sailor... one horse, the driver and sailor passenger were drowned... .

The worst tragedies of all also involved horses and carts. In June, 1846, six young men and three young women were riding on a cart which fell into a deep hole in a ford; they were all trapped and drowned. Eleven years later, the same cart was involved in another and greater tragedy. In 1857, it was loaned to 12 young men wanting to go to Lancaster Fair. Again, horse and cart plunged into a deep hole and all twelve were drowned. Quite possibly the deep hole in each case was where a flat-bottomed coasting vessel, a *flatt*, loaded with Furnessian iron ore and waiting for the tide, had been deliberately grounded in the stream. Lifting off with the next tide, it would leave a huge hole in the stream bed - unfortunately near the usual ford - which filling with water, left nothing to betray either size or depth.

Even today, the tide has a fearsome bore. This is yet another hazard, an advancing wave immediately preceding the flowing tide. Small in height (it can rarely exceed two feet), dependent on wind and whether it is a shallow neap or much deeper spring tide, it may sweep the unwary off their feet. The bore advances as fast as a sharp-pacing man can walk, rapidly filling gullies, making deep, uncrossable moats before and behind any unwary bather or walker on the wide sands. The rushing water creates temporary islands, to which the panic-stricken race, and where, if help is not coming in time, they are soon overwhelmed as the incoming tide grows deeper. The quicksands are plentiful, and almost every year some unwary person or persons is pulled away from a terrible death in these innocently surfaced, deadly traps for man or beast. Today, as in the past, the wide expanse of Morecambe Bay with its currents, bore and deadly sinking sands, is still a fearsome place to the ignorant, the over-confident, or the unwary.

Away from the Bay, safe from flood and rushing tide, the great Priory of Cartmel rises like some grey, primeval rock. Until its Dissolution, in 1536,

Cartmel Priory. Photo: Walt Unsworth

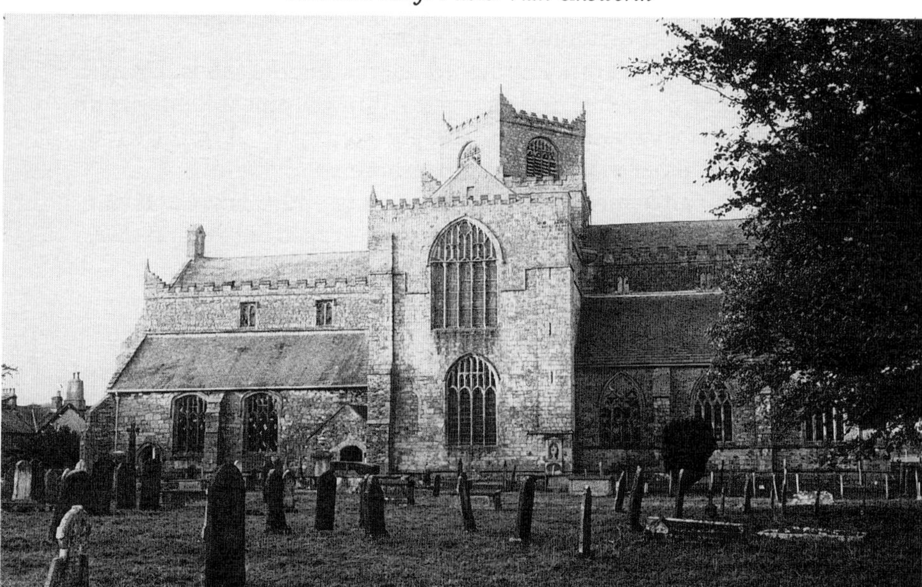

it was an Augustinian house, a place of dark-robed 'Black Canons'. They built the huge pile, the tall tower set unusually diagonally across its squared base. The whole building is of grey sandstone, a gritty material to the touch but a warm and pleasing tone in any sunlight. By its size, and position, towering above the village square, it seems very much out of place; massive and cathedral-like, overawing the equally ancient village, browbeating it, even when a host of noisy summer visitors crowd into and swamp the buildings crouching by the sturdy grey Priory walls.

Cartmel Priory was built about the end of the 12th century, and originally, complete with tithe barns and other outhouses, occupied a much greater area than it does today. It was sadly and brutally damaged after the Dissolution by the agents of Henry VIII and for a long time was not much more than a ruin, open to the sky. This perhaps, was in part-vengeance for the brave but foolhardy monks who had defied the king in that sad period after the Pilgrimage of Grace, 1537. This affair was an attempt by northern folk to save the monasteries and the old religion, but was eventually used as an excuse by Henry to wreak terrible punishment on those daring to defy him. Several of the Black Canons, plus some local laymen, were taken to Lancaster gaol and there hung, as a grim example *pour encourager les autres!* There is a local tale that these victims were hung from the arch of the ancient gateway which dominates the village square today, but it seems that Lancaster was the true place of such terrible execution.

Surprisingly, and eventually, the king allowed the local people to repair the Priory and use it as their church, but the pillaging, outrageous theft, and deliberate vandalism by and after the King's Commissioners was extensive. One great loss was the magnificent east window, where now much is plain glass. Some of the window, fortunately, has been preserved elsewhere, because the early church authorities of Bowness-on-Windermere bought many of the brightly coloured glass panels to embody in their own magnificent east window. The coats-of-arms of many local families, plus an unknown Prior of Cartmel and five canons (all named), two coats of arms of the Priory, and those of Lord Grey (an early 15th century patron of it) are all gloriously still present, though miles away from their original site.

There is still much to see and marvel at within the Priory, such as the 15th century misericords, the choir stalls, full of fascinating carving coupled with sly jest in wooden caricature. There is also the over-ornate tomb of the Yorkist Harrringtons and the sad marble effigy of the late Victorian Lord Frederick Cavendish. This appears on the north-western side of the nave, a marvellous example of monumental carving cut in Derbyshire stone. Poor Cavendish is part and parcel of the sad but continuing story of the Irish

'Troubles', for he was cruelly murdered in Phoenix Park, Dublin, in 1882; stabbed to death by so-called Irish patriots whilst trying to defend his friend and Parliamentary colleague. Equally sad evidence of trouble of an earlier time, but nothing like so magnificent, lies directly across the nave from the carving of poor Cavendish. This is a small door, set in the south wall and kept permanently locked. The ancient timbers bear several rounded holes, the mark of musket balls. These were fired in anger during the Civil War by local villagers incensed by sacrilegious Roundheads stabling their horses within this sacred place. Their anger is easily understood, for in this lovely old church, by tall pillars, before the altar lit by the huge east window, under the awesome pile of the tower, or indeed almost anywhere within its walls, one may feel something of the peace, calm and comfort given by Cartmel Priory to generations of Cartmel folk - and so many others - down the long, long years of its existence.

Less than two miles east of Cartmel and in complete contrast to the ageless serenity of the Priory, Grange-over-Sands is a charming combination of Victoriana and Edwardiana brought into being by the agency of the Furness Railway. It can be likened to a tiny Bournemouth, or perhaps a very small Torquay, but instead of being a retirement haven for Army and Navy officer-personnel, it was founded largely by wealthy mill-owners of Yorkshire and Lancashire wanting to spend their old age by the sea.

As the name suggests, it was once yet another grange, or outling farm of Cartmel Priory; the Victorians added the 'over Sands' bit to the title in order to attract a 'better class of visitor'. Sadly for this tiny town the Sands of the title (often thick, cloying mud) are now threatened by a comparatively new and apparently unstoppable menace. This is a tough, yard high maritime grass, *Spartina Anglica*, a fertile hybrid between native British species and an

Spartina Anglica - this rapidly spreading grass is taking over large areas of the shore at Grange

American alien accidentally introduced to this country more than a hundred years ago. At first slowly and now very rapidly, it is investing huge coastal areas of the 'Bay. It colonises the tidal mud, starting in the more sheltered areas and develops into an overwhelming prairie of waist-high grass. This slows down the incoming tide, which then releases any accumulated, tide-borne silt; so that gradually, millimetre by millimetre at first, the grass builds up the land. Eventually, all but the highest spring tides are kept below these grassy areas and in effect, the sea approaches the land less and less each year. The tidal water is receding more and more towards the 'Bay centre. *Spartina anglica*, unlike so many plant and animal hybrids, is very fertile. The grass increases season by season not only by vegetative means such as the rapid spread of adventitious roots through the mud, but also grows vigorously from scattered seeds - which, incidentally, have a high resistance to the normal plant-toxicity of salt sea water. Much time, and a lot of money are needed if Grange-over-Sands will live up to its old and proper title again.

Grange town, not much more than a hundred years old, remains neat and dignified. It has a handsome promenade alongside an attractive park bearing a small collection of wildfowl. These may include snow geese and Emperor geese from arctic Canada, Bar-headed geese from the edge of the Himalayas and Ne-ne geese from distant Hawaii. There are Ruddy shelduck from India, Wood and mandaraine ducks of unbelievable colour and beauty, pochard, with dark chestnut heads, and Roman-nosed handsome eiders - St Cuthbert's ducks. For the size of this place, the wildfowl collection is remarkable.

To stroll along by the sea here is to glimpse the tastes of a bygone age; a quieter and more restrained time when life appeared to be more dignified (mostly for the lucky, well-endowed few) but where everyone knew his or her proper place. I find Grange a delightful haven of quiet.

Two miles to the north-east, but well inland, close by the western bank of

The iron memorial to 'Iron-mad' Wilkinson at Lindale

Examples of Wilkinson's iron pipes are still to be seen at Wilson House, Lindale, where the iron master once had a foundry

the River Winster (which was the border between Lancashire North of the Sands and the old county of Westmorland) is Lindale. It is a scattered straggling, pleasant little village, with houses clustered down the length of steep hill. At the foot of this incline, a little to one side, on the road towards Grange, is a gigantic pillar of solid iron. This is the memorial to 'Iron-mad' John Wilkinson, outstanding pioneer of the Industrial Revolution. His former home, Castlehead, is situated on a tall crag rearing from a flat valley floor which was a peat-moss before he set to and drained it. The house, still in existence, was built on a site which yielded Roman artifacts of coin and pottery. This fascinating collection was lost years ago, but left behind much speculation that the site possibly held the northernmost Roman villa in the west. Wilson House, another former residence and foundry of the ironmaster, lies not far away. Unbelievably, the busy farmyard there has many of Wilkinson's famous iron pipes; cast originally as cylinders and skillfully bored out they litter the place, silent memorials to the sheer genius of the man who made them.

Somewhere in the steeply-sloping Lindale churchyard lies the body of Wilkinson in an iron coffin of his own design. He was buried *five* times, thus fulfilling the prophecy of a local 'wise woman'. First, body and coffin were temporarily lost in the sands of the Bay when bearers, bringing the body from Wilkinson's Bilston foundry, were overtaken by the tide. Extricated from the clinging sand, the coffin was then found to be too small to hold the final wooden and lead shells as directed by Wilkinson in his will. While a

Lindale Church where Wilkinson was finally buried - at the fifth attempt! The grave has unfortunately been lost

new and larger coffin was being cast, he was buried temporarily in the grounds of his Lindale home at Castlehead. His body was disinterred, transferred to the new coffin, and then, still in the Castlehead grounds, the grave was found to be too shallow before it hit solid rock! It was eventually buried deeper, and the iron memorial seen today, placed over it. When Castlehead changed hands within 20 years of Wilkinson's interment, the new owners objected to both grave and memorial, so poor John was disinterred once again! The huge iron memorial was finally transferred to its present site at the base of Lindale hill and John's body, ensconced in the famous iron coffin designed by himself, was buried at last in the steep grounds of Lindale churchyard. Details of the exact spot have long been lost, so that the man who was perhaps the most active ironmaster in all England in his day, lies in an unknown and unmarked grave somewhere in the grassy slope of the churchyard. Perhaps a carefully-used metal detector may pinpoint his last resting place some day; unless, of course, the iron-coffin has rusted away!

Printed in Great Britain by
Martin's of Berwick Ltd.